Early Praise for *Killer Presentation Skills*

"I'm a tough critic – especially when it comes to competitors – but *Killer Presentation Skills* is right on the mark. This is an excellent book for everyone who wants to take their presentation skills to the next level."

- Karen Friedman
Karen Friedman Enterprises
Author of *Shut Up and Say Something: Business Communication Strategies to Overcome Challenges and Influence Listeners*

"Most courtroom litigators make it all the way through college and law school without ever learning how to effectively speak to a group. I'm here to say that the client whose representation has not read this book has a fool for a lawyer!"

Suzanne Bender, ESQ.
Noted Philadelphia area Attorney

"In our business, presentations are all we do. And we have to do them right, because we're basically asking our prospects to trust us with their life savings. Over the years our firm has brought in numerous presentation "experts", but no method that we've ever seen comes close to Mr. Jefferys' program for creating an atmosphere of both comfort and complete trust for our audiences."

James Gallagher, CLTC
Creative Financial Group

"Whether you've been speaking for years or just starting out – you need to learn *"The Skills."* This book explains what you've been doing wrong and more importantly, how to change those behaviors for good. Your audiences will thank you."

Julie Terberg - Principal and Creative Director
Terberg Design LLC

"I speak to very large crowds - a thousand or more. I've had a pretty good reputation in my field for many years, but not so much as a great speaker. As Jefferys makes clear, speaking well is about acquiring certain behaviors, something anyone can do, and not about being born with a given talent. Now I'm known not for just for my expertise, but for my ability to grab and hold an audience. When I speak, people listen. I absolutely love what I do!"

-Geoffrey Katzenberg, MD

Killer
Presentation Skills

Other Works by J. Douglas Jefferys

And Your Point Is?

Techniques for Effective Presentations

Competitive Presentation Skills

Presentation Skills for Financial Advisors

The 95th Percentile

Killer Presentation Skills

How to acquire *The Skills*, and say goodbye to fear, sweat, and 'practice, practice, practice'!

J. Douglas Jefferys

PublicSpeakingSkills.com

PHILADELPHIA | LOS ANGELES | NEW ENGLAND

Killer Presentation Skills

by J. Douglas Jefferys

Copyright (c) 2011 J. Douglas Jefferys

All rights reserved. No part of this book may be reproduced or transmitted in any form or by any means, mechanical or electronic, to include photocopying, recording or by any data storage or retrieval system without written permission from the author, except for those provisions in U.S. Copyright Law, 2009 pertaining to previews, reviews or critiques.

Published by:

PublicSpeakingSkills.com, a dba of Autotrain.net, LLC
Chester Springs, PA 19425 USA

Library of Congress Control Number: 2011913461

ISBN-13: 978-0615499970 (PublicSpeakingSkills.com)
ISBN-10: 061549997X

Cover design: *Another contemplative work* by
The Navel Academy Press

Parts of this book were published in a previous work by the author, *And Your Point Is?* (Trafford, 2006) and have been significantly edited and updated for this publication. Any innaccuracies or perceived slights to individuals are inadvertent.

Please visit **www.publicspeakingskills.com** for information on other books, audio and DVD's on presentation delivery skills, presentation design skills, consultative selling and more.

This book available at quantity discounts for bulk purchases:
Please call: 888-663-7711

ACKNOWLEDGEMENTS

The author wishes to gratefully acknowledge the following people for their generous help and guidance in seeing this manuscript to fruition:

Tim Malloy, my business partner and head of our West Coast office who had to persevere at his own job whilst being constantly called upon to proofread and critique, chapter by chapter and concept by concept, until this work passed professional muster.

Claire Baillargeon, who, amongst her other stations in life looks after our New England office and helps us with all things French.

Deborah Meredith, the only person I know who both corrects me on my grammar and is correct when she does.

Our **Tens of Thousands of Participants**, who over the course of fifteen years of training helped as much as anyone to form and polish the content. They say there is no better way to learn than to teach, and I hope I have been a good enough student over the years to develop and modify our program to best serve your needs.

FOREWORD

It's been said that public speaking is the number one human fear. Whether true or not, in my years in business I have seen thousands of intelligent, successful, well spoken people turn to jelly when they stand up in front of a group and try to begin speaking.

It should not have to be this way.

The ability to present, to speak to others, is crucial in today's world. While the many advances in electronic communication have been staggering, I think you will agree with me that there is something lacking in our human interaction. We need to see and hear each other face to face to really communicate at the highest level as human beings.

Too much misunderstanding results from impulsive texting, poorly worded emails, deleted voice mails, and Facebook and Twitter posts. We must be able to stand up and speak with sincerity and confidence if success is to be achieved.

The book you now hold provides the simplest and easiest method ever developed to transform you from a speaking zero into a speaking hero. Using the "Lock, Talk and Pause" program, anyone with a modicum of desire can become a truly outstanding presenter.

When you learn and practice the techniques outlined in these pages, you will feel empowered, less stressed, and less anxious. You will be able to think, to remember the points to be covered. You will speak with more passion and belief, which means your audience will remain engaged, following you every step of the way.

And when this occurs, your audience, the most important component of your presentation, will leave saying, "I'm glad I was here today. This was a good use of my time."

And isn't that what you really want? When they're happy, you are happy.

I urge you to buy this book, to study the ideas presented. Within a short span of time and with a little practice, you can become the speaker you've always wanted to be.

Tim Malloy
Fall 2011

*Courage is what it takes to stand up and speak;
courage is also what it takes to sit down and listen.*

-- Winston Churchill

DEDICATION

To Barbara (who hates to be called that) simply for always believing in me. Some souls are with you for life.

"Be sincere; be brief; be seated."
~FDR, on speechmaking

Preface

Congratulations!

You've taken the first step to becoming one of a very select group of speakers in the world — those who have what is known in the speaking industry as "*The Skills*". People who get paid well to speak all share one of two traits: either they're famous, or they own "*The Skills*". To be able to move your audience, you must know how to keep them focused on you, engaged in your message, and thinking on the same page, every step of the way.

Keeping an audience with you every step of the way is simply not possible with the way most speakers behave when in front of a group. Most of us have been taught from an early age to speak in a way that sends the wrong signals to your audience — in many cases exactly the *opposite* of what you would like to signal. Worse, these standard behaviors actually reduce your cognitive capacity at the time you most desperately need it.

At PublicSpeakingSkills.com, we have been training people from business, politics, the military, and the clergy for over 15 years in *The Skills* you are about to discover. During that time, we have had the privilege to work with over 30,000 people from all walks of life, and here is what we have learned: 99% of speakers engage in *exactly* the same behaviors, and consequently produce similar results. In fact, in our onsite programs, we begin with an exercise that "benchmarks" how each student speaks before training. In every one of these exercises, we are able to predict *to the second* what each participant will do during their initial delivery. To the second!

The Skills can be learned

Most people present the way they do simply because they've never been shown the proper way. And though many people have learned public speaking in high school or college, that education tends to focus on *content* rather than *behaviors*. If you have taken such a class, it is likely your assignments were to create a series of speeches: The Informative, The Inspirational, The Motivational, etc. Sound familiar? But you likely were taught nothing about the actual delivery, other than to look at everyone in the audience and watch your umms and ahhs. Worse, you may even have received positive feedback for your speaking behaviors by people either too polite or simply not knowledgeable enough to tell you otherwise.

The good news is that you can learn to do it right. This book is about learning *The Skills* to deliver in a way that, no matter what the topic or tone or reason for your speaking, people will listen. This book will teach new speakers the right way, and it will help veteran speakers, who have not been effective, to vastly improve their presentation results.

This book will teach you to:

- Speak with authority
- Eliminate your natural anxiety, completely
- Understand what the audience expects from you
- Embrace the idea that it's okay to go into a presentation unrehearsed
- Feel comfortable with not knowing what you're going to say until just before you say it
- Accept that the most powerful thing you can say is sometimes nothing at all

In other words, this book will teach you *The Skills*.

The Skills are, indeed, a set of behaviors that you learn, and not something that you are born with. Very few people are 'born' with the ability to stir a group into action with their words. Those people have what the rest of us don't: it's called "charisma". Charismatics have been known to lead thousands to action by the power of their spoken words. But even people with very strong charisma need to study and practice *The Skills*.

For example, charisma alone didn't get Bill Clinton to the top job in the world. President Clinton was not always a great speaker. He had charisma, but he also had he brains to know that he did not know everything — and that becoming a great speaker was both essential to his job and something he could learn.

Clinton was one of only a handful of men elected as President of the United States without great personal or family wealth. He got elected because of his ability to motivate people to listen to him, work for him, follow him and support him all the way. He was successful because he didn't simply speak; he spoke (and still speaks) with a manner and a style that caused people to not only listen to his words but also to *hear* them, *remember* them, and to *believe* them.

Bill Clinton has *The Skills*.

The Skills supersede genes, culture, background, heritage, and to a large extent even education. People are not moved by messages delivered by speakers whom they don't feel are "real". And yet most of us were taught behaviors that cause us to adopt completely alien personas when we speak to groups. We try to become "Presenterman!" or "Presenterwoman!".

Killer Presentation Skills is more than just a book to read and hope that some of the principles sink in. Throughout the course of this book you will be given assignments to:

- Make daily observations of how other people speak and act
- Pay closer attention to your own physical actions when you speak
- Learn to employ *The Skills*

As you learn from this book (and because it's not a live class) you will be drawing upon people that you engage every day as your unwitting, surrogate coaches. Don't worry - you won't be doing anything unethical, dishonest, or remotely manipulative! These people will act as your coaches by allowing you to see yourself in them, and then becoming aware of behaviors that work either for you or against you when you speak.

By practicing the exercises at the end of each chapter, you will be prepared to fully comprehend and appreciate the next chapter. By the end of the book, you will be ready to walk into your next presentation and perform at a level considerably higher than where you are now.

How much better you get is entirely up to you. You will continue to improve with every presentation you give. That's not true of all skills you can acquire. When it comes to speaking, you can look forward to not only a lifetime of improvement, but also to an activity that becomes ever more enjoyable with every small improvement you make.

"Action speaks louder than words but not nearly as often."
- Mark Twain

*"Be who you are
And say what you feel,
Because those who mind
Don't matter,
And those who matter
Don't mind."*

-Dr. Seuss

Contents

Part 1: Physical Behaviors

    Chapter 1: A Wiring Problem   11

    Chapter 2: Seeing Eye to Eye   27

    Chapter 3: Lock, Talk & Pause   39

    Chapter 4: The Power of the Pause   55

    Chapter 5: Putting Passion in Your Pitch   69

Part II: Presentation Content

    Chapter 6: Organizing Your Presentation   89

    Chapter 7: Introduction to Design   105

    Chapter 8: The 7 Rules of Visual Design   125

    Chapter 9: Applying the Rules   147

Part III: Putting it All Together

    Chapter 10: Stand and Deliver   167

    Chapter 11: The Dreaded Q & A   181

*"Without effective delivery, a
speech of the highest mental
capacity can be held in no esteem
while one of the moderate abilities,
with this qualification, may surpass
even those of the highest talent."*

- Cicero

Part I:
Physical Behaviors

"Of all the talents bestowed upon men, none is so precious as the gift of oratory. He who enjoys it wields a power more durable than that of a great king. He is an independent force in the world."

- Sir Winston Churchill

Chapter 1:
A Wiring Problem

Mark Twain said, *"There are two types of speakers: those that are nervous and those that are liars."* Twain once disliked speaking (something he had done earlier in life) so much that when, later in life, facing bankruptcy from a series of bad investments, he initially refused his friends' advice that he take to the road and give talks.

Eventually, as his pride caught up with him, he did just that: on a road that would take him to China and Japan — twice — and allow him to retire not only debt-free but moderately wealthy. But he didn't go without first becoming a student of public speaking in an effort to find what made good speakers good.

As it turns out, what was true in Mark Twain's time is still true today. When people are asked to list their greatest fears, here's how it shakes out:

Flying	18%
Death	19%
Sickness	19%
Deep Water	22%
Financial Problems	22%
Insects & Bugs	22%
Heights	32%
Public Speaking	**41%**

These numbers come from *The Book of Lists*, 1991, but it's been pretty much the same since they first started asking the question. When people are asked to list their greatest fears, speaking to a group always filters to the top. In fact, as you can see, speaking to a group ranks twice as high as death.

Jerry Seinfeld reportedly said of this list that it suggests at a funeral, the person giving the eulogy....would rather be in the box!

That's funny, unless it's you giving the eulogy. But why do you become afraid when speaking in public?

The answer is that when you find yourself in front of a group of people, your neo-cortex, which acts as a "first responder" in a complex nervous system that was hard wired eons ago to "protect" you, reads the situation as the classic threat scenario of being *one-against-many*. And anytime the system finds itself in a one-against-many situation, there are only two ways we can respond: stand and fight or run like hell - the classic fight-or-flight response. You do indeed feel exactly the same way when faced with a truly life-threatening event. If you are afraid when speaking before a group, it's because the very same chemicals that are released when you blow out a tire at 70 miles per hour are coursing through your veins and signaling that you feel afraid.

> **Essential Point:** People have difficulty speaking in public for the simple reason that humans are just not wired to do so! The one-against-many scenario brings on a physiological response to which there are only *two* available responses, and "negotiating" is not one of them! Attempts to "believe" there is a third path – something other than fighting or fleeing – typically end in failure because the forces of logic and reason (or 'positive thinking') are not as strong as the manipulations of adrenaline.

When faced with the prospect of standing up and speaking in front of people, three processes, intertwined with each other, actually take hold of your systems, and often don't let go until well after the event that triggered them has ended.

The first thing that happens is the well-evolved thinking parts of your brain recognize a *potential* threat in the situation, but because at this moment you're not hard-wired to discern between the imagined and the real, your neo-cortex errs on the side of caution. It sends a clear signal to your hypothalamus, an almond-sized gland located in the center of your brain. The gland begins sending out hormones to prepare the body to deal with the threat. The signal to the hypothalamus takes milliseconds, and sometimes the brain is able to resolve the threat just as quickly. Unfortunately at this point a chain of events has started that takes considerably longer to subside.

You know how this works if you've ever been startled by someone approaching you from an unseen direction who is suddenly, unexpectedly, in your face. You jump, and then just as quickly realize that the person represents no threat to you whatsoever. But just try telling that to your heart. Often for minutes after the "threat" has been "resolved", you're still shaking, and you might even harbor somewhat ill feelings for the person who startled you, keeping your heart beating at a faster-than-normal rate and pounding with much more force than usual.

Fight or Flight

When the hypothalamus, which regulates most bodily functions, receives the threat signal, it sends a group of hormones to the pituitary gland at the base of your brain. This in turn releases hormones that activate your adrenal glands, which sit on top of your kidneys — a spot ideally centralized in the body to make for the shortest trip to all parts of the body for the adrenals' output: adrenaline.

Adrenaline is actually pretty cool stuff. It causes a number of responses in the body, all of which are designed to give your body the physical edge it needs to run like hell or stay and fight to the death. It starts with the heart.

First, adrenaline increases the rate at which your heart beats, speeding the process of moving blood through the oxygenating function of the lungs. Next, it increases the force of your heart's contractions, to ensure blood gets to the far reaches of your body like your fighting hands or your running feet. That's where the thump-thumps come from. All's pretty good so far.

Then, to make sure all these muscle groups are working best, adrenaline facilitates what is essentially a valving process that ensures enough blood is flowing to the *motor control* sections of your brain. Bit of a downside to this process, however, in that the system has to get the blood from somewhere, and finds the most convenient supplies in the *thinking* portions of your brain.

So just when the rational parts of your brain, which actually do not fear imminent death at the podium, want to have as much cognitive ability as they can muster, greater forces have other plans. You actually get a little bit dumber.

To take this one step farther, every time the brain finds itself in a situation where it feels threatened, not only does it send the reaction juices flowing, it also creates a little file in your brain. It's called a fear memory and is designed to give you a head start the next time it recognizes you're in a similarly "dangerous" situation.

You see, a long time ago, one of our ancestors was walking across the savannah; and out from the tall grass leapt this giant saber-toothed tiger. Instantly, our ancestor went into fight-or-flight mode, being the fastest young man in the tribe, was able to escape and make it home free.

Two weeks later, the ancestor, being fast but not too bright, went for a walk in the same part of the savannah.

This time, though, he was armed with something he didn't even know he had: a file in his brain that we refer to as a fear memory. And the information in that fear memory included the sounds that the tiger made rustling the grasses just before he jumped out. Armed with that pre-knowledge that a similar danger was lurking, the ancestor had a head start in getting out of there fast.

It works like this: If it's the first time your brain has been presented with a particular threat, it creates a new file. If it finds that there already is a file by that name (such as, say, publicspeakingfear.mem), then it overwrites it with the new experience. In any case, it writes to the file, and says, "Okay, next time you find yourself in a similar situation, we've got to start the fight-or-flight process."

When most people speak, they are not just working with the reality and repercussions that it's *one-against-many*. They are working from their fear memory file. One that probably goes back to grade school. Ever since your first experience with a sea of faces staring back at you while you tried to fake out your first stand-up book report, you've been modifying that file.

And any time you didn't have so elevated me overwhelmingly positive response, you've modified that file to give you a little bit more juice, then a little bit more, and a little bit more. So today, you start off any speaking engagement at an elevated — sometimes an extremely elevated — fear level.

You've got the fever

If all that weren't enough, adrenaline works to speed up

your metabolism as it works to turn glucose [blood sugar] into glycogen, the form of 'energy' your cells can use. This speed-up produces a couple of side effects, one being the perception of time slowing down. In fact, most umms and ahhs come from your wanting to fill the void of a perceived extended silence when the actual interval between your thoughts and words is in reality rather short.

If any of you has ever been in car accident or any event where you've faced real, imminent danger, you probably are familiar with how time seemed to s-l-o-w d-o-w-n. That's adrenaline speeding you up, so your perception of time is skewed.

More immediately noticeable is increased body temperature, which can manifest itself in the "cooling" process known as sweating. But that's not fair! Weren't you told never to let them see you sweat? And because burning all that glucose is a de-hydrative process, it can cause your mouth to go dry, which is often compounded when the facility puts out gallon jugs of water in front of every audience member but none at the podium.

Finally, whenever we send out a hormone there's always an anti-hormone emitted to keep it company. In the case of the adrenals we're talking nor-adrenaline. Nor-adrenaline's effect is to increase blood pressure, which you typically feel in the form of flushness in the face.

So if you've ever found yourself about to give a talk and felt your heart beating a little faster, with a discernible thump-thump, thump-thump, and your brain was a little less sharp than it should be — and stuck in a minor time warp; if you've ever felt moistness in your palms or around the collar and your face a bit flushed, then great! Your body is performing precisely to spec!

What you need to take home here is the understanding that, no matter what you may be consciously thinking, your sympathetic nervous system will always respond to external stimuli in the way it is hard-wired to do. Every time. That is why so much advice on overcoming the fear of public speaking is worthless. No amount of "positive thinking" or alternate perceived realities such as NLP "therapy" will cause your body to respond to an outside threat differently.

As long as you expose yourself to certain stimuli, your body's response will be the same. It is why our species has survived this long.

Sounds depressing, huh?

Well, this book would not exist if there weren't good news to impart. And that is, although you cannot change your response to certain stimuli, you certainly can change the type and frequency of the stimuli to which you expose yourself. It is this process that is at the heart of *The Skills*, and the initial steps to achieve it will constitute your first set of exercises.

"All our knowledge has its origins in our perceptions."
— Leonardo da Vinci

Three Simple Truths to Acquiring *The Skills*

In order to be a top presenter, remember these three:

1. If you're working too hard, you're doing it wrong.
2. It's not about you – it's all about them.
3. People *START* listening only when you *STOP* talking.

Truth #1:

If you're working too hard, you're doing it wrong.

Most presenters, until they are taught differently, try to do too many things at once Way too many things.

And the more they try to do, the harder their involuntary nervous systems have to work. But your body cannot respond quickly to conflicting actions.

The results are usually a loss of cognitive control, which is often not a good thing in the presence of your boss or colleagues. Can you relate to the following situations?

You're at a meeting with company associates who don't know each other. The meeting leader suggests you each tell the group your name, what you do for the company, and perhaps what you most want to take away from the meeting. You feel things happening in your body as you sense your turn is coming, and you feel a little uncomfortable. When it's your turn, you stand up and speak for a minute or two, then sit down. A moment later you can't remember a single word you said!

Or: You have been asked to make an impromptu speech at a dinner or meeting. When you get on your feet you suddenly can't think of a thing to say. You freeze, and the initial anxiety you felt when looking out at the group is suddenly compounded by the fear that you will be viewed as an idiot!

The latter example is generally caused not by your having *nothing* to say, but rather by your finding yourself with a half-dozen things to say, yet unable to decide which *one* thing would be best. Instead of prioritizing one, you were trying to juggle six!

As we'll see, not only does your brain seem to let you down when you need it most, but presenters then go on to exacerbate the problem by engaging in counter-productive behaviors, which for the most part include trying to do too many things at once. The only way you can take back control of your nervous system is to learn to do *one thing at a time*. You'll learn how to do this in the next chapter, but have faith that everyone can learn how to "uni-task". You will learn to undo your lifelong education of multi-tasking when its time to get up in front of a group.

You may think that working harder is better. Endemic to many cultures is the concept that *"All good things come from hard work"*, or *"There are no shortcuts to success"*. With public speaking, this is not the case.

Consider the Q&A portion of a speech. Many people see this as the scariest part of presenting because, unlike the prepared part of your talk, you don't know what's coming. But think of people who appear calm and collected during an interview or press conference – the former Defense Secretary Donald Rumsfeld comes to mind. "Rummey" had *The Skills*. And people with *The Skills* understand that speaking events need not necessarily be scripted in order to work. Attempting to plan everything you're going to say, or believing you must have your words completely planned out ahead of time is an example of working too hard.

> **Essential Point:** Sometimes it's best *not* to rehearse or preplan, but to go with what comes to you at the moment. For that to work, however, you must understand you can always think clearly in the moment when you are focused only on the *very* next moment. You cannot, as most speakers do, try to focus on the next, and the next, and the next - the string of moments thereafter.

Chapter 2 will show you how to not work so hard. You will break down the process into individual steps and then devote your attention to each of those steps *one at a time*. And you will learn when (and only when) to begin thinking of what you want to say next, without having rehearsed it beforehand.

Truth #2:

It's not about you; it's all about them.

Whether it's the way they engage the audience with their eyes, what they do (or don't do) with their hands, or the pace with which they crank out the word stream, most of the behaviors in which speakers engage tend to work against both their own comfort level and the audience's ability to absorb what is being said.

In Chapter 3, you will observe what presenters do with their arms and hands. Instead of using motion to throw off excess energy, they tend to lock arms in a position that traps energy in a circulating loop. This rigid body-language can actually create a lose-lose situation, as it works to trap excess energy in the presenter's body while transmitting a contagious feeling of discomfort to the audience. You may feel more comfortable locked in a tight self-hug, but the audience actually feels less comfortable as it empathizes with your apparent anxiety or insecurity.

When you employ the behaviors that comprise *The Skills*, not only are you more relaxed, authoritative and convincing, but your audience has a much easier time hearing, seeing, and ultimately agreeing with the message you are trying to impart. As Yale's Professor Edward Tufte points out, "audiences are lazy, and audiences are fragile". You can't ask audiences to *work* to understand your message because they won't. And you can't make them feel uncomfortable or they'll spend what small amount of energy they have trying to get comfortable and won't have anything left to comprehend your point.

Equally important, if not more so, as the words of your message is *how* you speak. Proper eye-contact, gesturing, tone, volume and inflection - when done right all work to make for a great experience for both speaker and listeners alike.

Truth #3:

People only START listening when you STOP talking.

This is an easy concept to understand, but a tough one to master. Generally, people don't so much hear what is *being* said as they hear what was *just* said. In fact, the left hemisphere of your brain, where speech and text are processed, is programmed not to absorb information immediately, but rather to analyze it before storing or acting on it. It's a momentary process to be sure, but one that is considerably enhanced when a moment or two of silence follows an important message. Chapter 4 will impress upon you the importance of giving time for the audience to absorb your words.

Here's a great example: think what happens when someone tells a joke. Jokes usually are structured to lead the listener along an expected path, and the humor comes when the listener realizes that the punch-line has altered that path in an unexpected way. But you don't laugh at the moment the punch-line is delivered. You laugh only after you realize your line of thought has been diverted, which takes a moment or, if the joke is really good, two. You only hear what was actually said when the joker stops talking and your mind has the opportunity to recognize the misdirection.

Most speakers continue on with an endless stream of verbiage from the moment they open their mouths until they discover that the talk is over and they can (*Thank God!*) take their seats again. Once people start talking in front of a group it is difficult to get them to stop.

They've taught themselves to believe that as long as they continue to hear words coming out of their mouths, they are OK. A common fear is that somehow that stream will stop and they won't be able to get it started again.

But why is this so?

Remember, because of the physiological changes that occur in the body when you are facing an audience (adrenaline flow), your perception of time actually slows down. The universe doesn't change - your perception does. So although the audience is listening to you in real time, you perceive even a momentary lapse in your word-stream to be much longer that it actually is. And so a one-second pause for the audience might feel like three or four to you. As we mentioned, this is where umm's and ahh's are born. We hear that dreaded silence, and in a desperate need to fill it immediately, we grab for the closest thing — a non-word that easily fits into our word track.

It might be hard to believe, but time actually goes by quite nicely on its own, even when it's not filled with your words!

And there's value in it for you as well. Offering this pause to the audience doubles as your opportunity to think of the next thing to say. More on that note in Chapter 4.

Points to Remember

- Public speaking is a common fear. You are not alone.
- Increased heart beat, decreased intelligence, slowed time perception, sweating, dry mouth and a flushed face are all normal bodily reactions to fear.
- Working *less* will improve your outcome.
- You must give your audience time to absorb each point before moving on to the next.

Suggested Exercises

Modern presentation theory espouses a conversational approach to presenting, because that's the way to maximize both comfort and trust between you and the audience. The conversational approach, a modern refinement of the humanist style first made popular in western cultures by President John F. Kennedy, is quite a bit different from the oratory style that most people associate with earlier great speakers such as Winston Churchill and FDR.

The foundation of the conversational approach is proper eye contact, and the nature of that eye contact is quite unlike the way ninety-nine percent of presenters practice. In fact, after you know what to look for, you will discover what first differentiates those who have *The Skills* from those who don't is the way they engage their audiences with their eyes. Make no mistake: proper eye contact is only one component of *The Skills*, but when you understand exactly how you *must* look at your audience to be a great speaker, the other components tend to fall into place.

When you nail down these (surprisingly straightforward) eye contact techniques, you can deliver to a group of 500 without ever feeling more anxiety than you would when discussing your job to friends around a lunch table. Most people find that hard to believe until they've actually received training in *The Skills* (as your doing by reading this book), but when you get it, it's rather powerful stuff!

These exercises sound simple enough, but they do require a bit of vigilance on your part to have the desired effect. You must practice them *at every opportunity* in the coming days. Only once you have practiced these exercises will you know what you need to in order to move on to the next level of acquiring *The Skills*.

1. Observe others' eye contact. In every situation in which you interact with others, watch their eyes. Observe how long they maintain eye contact while they are speaking to you. Watch how they maintain eye contact while speaking to others. As often as you can, count the number of seconds they maintain continuous eye contact before switching to a new target and note this, preferably in a log of some sort.

2. In situations where someone is speaking to a group, count the number of seconds the speaker maintains eye contact with each individual. Determine what the average amount of time is. Log it.

Chapter 2:
Seeing Eye to Eye

In Western cultures, we tend to associate direct eye contact with telling the truth, and looking away - eye avoidance - with *not* telling the truth. If we want to know if somebody's telling the truth, we ask them to look us in the eye. We expect people to look us in the eye when they answer a direct question. With the possible exception of Presidents of the United States, it's very difficult for humans to just look someone in the eye — and lie.

A few years ago we were invited through a friend to attend a dinner at one of the most respected (read: expensive) restaurants in the area. The price was our having to sit through a financial presentation on retirement strategies. Although we didn't really want to go, we were tempted by the food and the fact that we probably wouldn't get there on our own dime anytime soon. Dinner was excellent, but when the time came for the spiel, our host stood up and instead of addressing any particular individual, looked directly at the vase in the center of the table the entire time he spoke! Sometimes he would look at the flowers, then scan to the creamer, then back to the flowers and on to the water jug. This man was trying to tell us how we should divest ourselves of most of our worldly liquid assets and invest them with him. He wanted us to literally trust him with our life savings. And yet he could not look us in the eye for even a moment when he spoke!

When dessert was served he passed around a sign-up sheet for the guests to fill-out and let him know when the most convenient time to meet with him would be. Keep in mind all fourteen of us had been treated to a meal and drinks that would easily exceed $150 each, the staff had treated us like royalty, and we were all feeling grateful to our host for the feast. But as you might imagine, not one of the fourteen guests signed up.

The host couldn't believe it! Here he had lavished us with this divine spread and no one was going to come through. Things began to get uncomfortable in the small room until we decided to put our name down.

At the appointment, we informed the host that we were not going to invest any money with him, but because we realized the generous dinner had been a financial flop, we would be happy to invest an hour of our time with him and teach him a bit about how to establish trust with his audience. The financial guy had other problems, too, but the result was the same: people have a hard time trusting people who can't or don't look them in the eye, especially when the slightest element of trust is at stake.

Making Observations

Have you taken the time to complete the exercises from Chapter 1 and have had opportunities to observe people talking to groups? If not, we strongly suggest you do so. Your maximum benefit will come from building on actual observations of what people do when they speak. It's important to observe objectively what they do with their eyes, what they do with their hands, and how they stand when they speak.

You should also pay attention to the speed at which words come out of their mouths, and listen to their volume and inflection. By volume we mean the amount of air passing through the larynx, and inflection being changes in pitch and tone. Finally, listen for non-words — those umms and ahhs and y'knows and so forth — that many people use to fill up any dead airtime.

In our on-site corporate classes, we videotape participants as they get up in front of the class and tell us a little bit about themselves. For most people, videotaping is a real eye-opener, especially if they have never seen themselves present before. In fact, with the chemical fear soup coursing through your brain, it's almost impossible to get any kind of handle on what you look like on the outside when speaking. The advantage of videotape is that we see speakers differently on screen than we do when watching them live. Humans filter out a lot of what cameras do not.

It's this unfiltered look at what participants actually do that provides the first epiphany to the difference that having *The Skills* makes when facing a group. And as we hinted last chapter, the most noticeable component of *The Skills* is eye contact.

What did you discover while observing other's eye contact as they spoke to you? Were you able to find an average time they looked at you before breaking off? What about the time people spent holding eye contact at any one person or object when speaking to groups? Before you consciously studied eye contact, would you have assumed that the time people held eye contact would be so short?

Aerosol Eyes (Or, Just a Second, Please)

"Look at everyone in the audience." Just about everybody has heard this bit of advice sometime in their public speaking education. And it's true; when you get up and speak in front of a group, you want to look to everyone in the audience. In very large groups, where it might be physically impossible to actually have eye contact with every individual, your goal is to have everyone in the audience *believe* that you were actually looking at them. More on this later.

Although most of us were told *what* to do, we were never really told *how* to do it. As a result, whenever we see people speak for the first time, we observe the phenomenon that we call "Aerosol Eyes".

It looks like this: the speaker gets up in front of the room and immediately begins to spray the audience with his vision. Back and forth, back and forth, rarely holding eye contact for more than one second at a time. After fifteen years of videotaping class participants (over 30,000 people) that is the average — one second. And it's often less than that.

To see what this looks like, go to:

www.publicspeakingskills.com/cato/Aerosol.wmv

You might have noticed in your observations that some people don't hold eye contact at all. When speaking to groups, some people tend to look down the whole time (hoping there are notes on the podium or the floor). Sometimes they look up to the heavens (hoping they'll find divine inspiration). As we'll see, that behavior is a rather common conditioned response to what people find difficult to deal with when their vision is in the "plane of the eyeballs".

If you observed speakers who avoided eye contact, how did that make you feel? Did you find it affecting the way you felt about what they were saying? How did it make you feel about yourself?

There are some people who have been taught that it is disrespectful to look others directly in the eye. But even in cultures where there are rules for eye contact based on social hierarchy, the exceptions are when one is teaching or when one wants to know he is being told the truth.

But for the most part, speakers tend to sweep back and forth, unwittingly sending out all the wrong signals, while exacerbating the fight-or-flight process already started when they stood to face the group to begin with.

What the Speaker Sees

Aerosol Eyes causes a number of problems. Every time you look to a new person in the audience, you force your brain to take in a new field of view. When it moves to a new field, your brain has to recalculate what it's seeing. And doing that once a second, repeatedly, when your body is already tense, you quickly reach a state of visual over-stimulation.

When you spray the audience as you speak, you ask your brain to take in and process way too much information per unit time. Remember, in this situation of one-against-many, your brain is in its threat calculation mode, and every time you ask it to process a new scene, it also has to perform a new threat calculation.

Each time you frame a new image, your brain processes whole new groups of information: you're picking up the color of the audience member's clothes, the look in her eyes, the hunch of his shoulders. You're registering his countenance. You're trying to decide: is this person going to jump across his seat, come up here and try to kill me? Do I have to kill him first, or would it be best to try to run away?

And pretty soon — performing the visual threat calculations and recalculations once a second — you find yourself in a state of visual and mental over-stimulation. You just get too much. Every single time you change your field of view, your brain automatically takes in everything, and must perform a new calculation. It has to. That's its job.

Then think about this: All that energy your brain is using to process these visual assaults you're throwing at it, how much do you suppose is left to do the job you really want it to – to form the thoughts and words that make up your presentation? You're working too hard! And that means you're violating Rule #1.

What the Speaker Feels

During the calculation and recalculation process, blood is draining from the thought-processing centers of your brain in order to feed the motor control sections. Your body's priority at this point is preparing to either fight or flee. Not trying to appear poised and intelligent and well-prepared for your boss in the back of the room. Is it any wonder that you so often lose your train of thought?

We'll say it again: *No amount of logic, reasoning, or positive attitude training is going to change the way your body responds when you subject your brain to the repeated stimuli of looking at a new face every second.*

> **Essential Point:** Don't set yourself up for certain failure by believing you can change a hard-wired physiological process by thinking nice thoughts. We're huge believers in the power of positive thinking. Think positively about this: you can change the result by changing a few behaviors. But you *cannot change your body's chemistry.*

People who appear calm and collected or even enjoying themselves when facing a large audience don't appear that way because they have more inner strength than you or because they have more self-discipline or are better at conquering their weaknesses. They feel competent and confident because they don't have nature's fear juice surging through their veins. And they do that by simply not subjecting themselves to the stimuli that causes the fight-or-flight reactions! How? Simple: to start, they use appropriate eye contact techniques; *they don't scan.*

Speakers with *The Skills* know that they can not remain calm and connected while scanning the room at 60 PPM (people per minute). They know that they are working way too hard if they try to speak and do that, too. They know that if they're working too hard, they're doing it wrong. They know that they need virtually all of their cognitive ability to form the next cohesive, well-structured thought. And so they don't scan.

The takeaway, then, is this: You can not change the way your body will react to a given stimuli, but you can easily change the type and volume of the stimuli to which you subject it.

What the Audience Sees

If it weren't bad enough that the *presenter* gets all screwed up while trying to process way too much visual information at once, the very same behavior — Aerosol Eyes — creates problems for the *audience,* too.

Here's where it starts to get serious. The problems for the audience start when a speaker sends this message to the group:

"Hi! I'm glad that all of you were able to be here today.

"What I'm here to tell you is this: that for the next 45 minutes, I'm never going to have any contact with any one of you as individuals at all. In fact, as I'm up here spewing back and forth into the ether, I don't see you as individuals — I see you as just this big amorphous blob. Okay? You are not really people, per se. You're never going to be called to task. I'm never going to know whether you're really paying attention or not.

"So this might be a good time to crank up Solitaire or break out those Blackberries and just take a few steps back from this whole program!"

And that's the message that you send — you literally give the audience *permission* to drop back a level or two. You let them know that, instead of being participants in an interactive event, they are merely observers to a performance by someone who doesn't really know or care whether they're with the program. In other words, we create and foster a real lack of connection.

Average speakers have trained most groups to think of a presentation as something where they are indeed observers to a performance. As such, most people who come to the presentation will settle into a removed state. Consider the last time you gave a presentation. As you spoke, did you find some people who were actually looking away, taking notes, working on their laptops, or anything other than devoting attention to you? How did that make you feel? Did it help your confidence, or do you think it might have actually added to your anxiety level, even if you weren't 'consciously' aware of it?

That doesn't happen to people who have *The Skills*.

The audience never sees quite the level of discomfort that you yourself might feel, but your anxiety still emanates to a large degree. They may notice the nervous twitter in your hands or the slightest quiver in your voice, or the way your arms are locked around your torso as your lower body moves around in poorly orchestrated dance steps.

What the Audience Feels

When you appear nervous, everybody in the audience is reminded of one thing: at least *they're* not up there. They know that speaking in front of a group is something that they fear more than death or taxes.

They don't necessarily *sympathize* with you, but they do *empathize* with you. They know what you as a speaker are feeling. Unfortunately, your anxiety is contagious. This empathy that the audience feels for you turns into anxiety. And your audience becomes uncomfortable.

> **Essential Point:** In order to impart any new information to a group, you first have to make them comfortable. That's why companies that can afford it send their people off to resorts or retreats to conduct their training. They go to places that are separated from the anxieties and hassles of the real world, where their every creature comfort and basic need is looked after and where they can be as comfortable as possible.

When it comes to pursuing our need for knowledge, we humans fall trap to Maslow's Hierarchy of Needs. That is, before we are susceptible to uptake of new information, our basic physiological needs must first be satisfied. Any deficiencies in fulfillment of our basic needs must be addressed before we can move to a higher level. As a result, we tend not to listen to anything unless and until all our basic needs are taken care of. As advanced as a species we think we all are, in the end, we are again ruled by primitive instincts that most humans find impossible to overcome.

If you're cold, you're thinking about how to get warm. If you're too warm, you're thinking about how to get cool. If you're hungry or thirsty, you're thinking about that. If your buttocks are sore, you're thinking about when you'll get to stand up. If your bladder's full, you wonder when the next break is coming so can hit the restroom. You've been there, right?

Anything you do to make an audience feel uncomfortable gets them thinking about something *other* than your program. And if you want to achieve true knowledge transfer, which is what a presentation is all about, then you (the speaker) must be on the same page – indeed the same wavelength - as every individual in the audience, every step of the way. You can't give them any reason to think of anything other than your message.

So to ensure that your audience is comfortable, *you* must feel comfortable, and you must *look* comfortable. That's simply not possible with Aerosol Eyes.

Points to Remember

- Spraying the audience with eye contact increases the frequency your body will react to new fear stimuli.
- Most cultures translate inability to look someone in the eye as not telling the truth.
- Your discomfort and anxiety is contagious; your audience will internalize it and stop listening.

Suggested Exercises

1. When you speak with others this week — whether it is to friends over the lunch table, giving input during a meeting, or making a presentation of any length — be conscious of your own eye contact.

    When speaking with someone, do you stay focused on them? Do you look up, away, or down while speaking? Or do you maintain eye contact the entire time you are speaking with someone? How often do you move away from eye contact and then return? Do you look at other people for the same amount of time when talking to one as when you are talking to many?

"Do the thing you fear and the death of fear is certain."

\- Ralph Waldo Emerson

Chapter 3:
Lock, Talk & Pause

The most common reason people don't look at members of the audience directly is because they're too busy trying to manage all the aspects of the presentation at one time. They try to run the whole company – doing all the jobs for all the different departments at once.

First, they try to run the Design department. That's where the ideas and the words are created. They try to run Manufacturing, where the words are produced and spit out of the mouth as part of a never-ending conveyer belt of half-sentences and appended phrases. And if that weren't enough, they try to run Distribution, where every second they must deliver the goods to a new customer, back and forth across the room. Phewwww!

You can't design, manufacture and distribute your words all at the same time and expect the quality of your product to be any good.

Instead, you need to do only one thing at a time: it's a process we call *Lock, Talk, and Pause*.

Lock, Talk and Pause involves the speaker's actually engaging i-n-d-i-v-i-d-u-a-l-s in the audience, one at a time. Engaging people one at a time is something that we *are* equipped for, and something that doesn't by any physiological pre-wiring cause us much anxiety. It's as simple as this:

- *Lock* eyes with one person
- *Talk* to that person through the completion of a single thought
- *Pause* before engaging the next person

> **Essential Point:** From this day forward, you will never again speak to a group of individuals; you will speak only to the individuals in a group. So when you're speaking, deliver your speech as a series of one-on-one conversations. Remember: If your eyes aren't locked, your jaw *must* be. If you've got words to say, you need to say them to a set of eyeballs — one person at a time.

The hardest part of this process for most people is to learn how to stop talking. This, by far, takes the most effort for people to grasp. It's easy to learn to maintain eye contact for more than a second. It's much more difficult to learn to pause at the end of every thought. Yet you need to pause to give your audience the chance to actually hear what you just said. More on this later.

The 80% Solution

In our onsite classes, we have participants practice holding eye contact for five seconds. We have people get up and tell us a story about a time in their life that provided a lasting memory. We have audience members hold up their hands, and as the speaker is telling his story, the audience member to whom he's speaking is counting to herself: five, four, three, two, one. And when the audience member gets to one, when the speaker's actually maintained continual eye contact for a minimum of five seconds, she puts her hand down.

At that point, the speaker knows he has completed the minimum five seconds of direct eye contact, and the speaker now has 'permission' to finish what he's saying, pause, and move on to the next person. We practice a hold of five seconds, not because there's any such thing as a five-second rule, but because it's five times longer than the average untrained speaker typically looks at any one person. Think about this: in going from one second to five seconds, the presenter reduces the amount of visual stimulation his brain receives and must process by eighty per cent!

In the beginning of a presentation, when most presenters are subconsciously still processing every new frame of view for its threat potential, this can mean an 80% reduction in the amount of adrenaline called up. That's a difference that our participants can physically feel, and it often produces their first epiphany regarding *The Skills*.

But let us repeat: there is no such thing as a five-second rule, or any other set time period for holding eye-contact. [If you had to keep track of seconds as well as your words, that would be doing more than one thing at a time, a clear violation of Rule #1] What's important is to hold eye contact through your entire thought, no matter how long that thought might be. It might be quite simple and last as little as two seconds. It might be more involved and take as long as eight to ten seconds to get out. But whatever the length, don't split the thought between two or more individuals because then you'd also be doing more than one thing at a time — speaking your words and finding a new target.

Think of your words as bullets, and for safety's sake, lock on to your target *before* you pull the trigger.

So maintaining eye contact longer significantly reduces the amount of the crank-me-up that your brain experiences. You've reduced the amount of signals that the hypothalamus is sending down to the adrenals that say, *"More power, Scotty. Pump me up. I need more!"*

In going from an average of one second of eye-contact to five seconds, your body is receiving only 20% of the chemicals that your insular cortex is interpreting as fear. At this point your conscious mind is actually experiencing a totally different bodily response from what is has been used to. Many participants in our classes tell us that they can feel the physical difference after completing only of few of the exercises we perform during the training day.

This is not about changing your belief system. This is nothing more than your changing the stimuli to which you expose yourself and having your body react the way it is hard-wired to do. This is what is so powerful about *The Skills*.

Talking to Individuals

So the process goes like this: You find a target and lock eyeballs. You deliver a complete thought to that one person. Then you do the hardest part — you pause. You pause before turning to the next person, and speak to the next person through your next thought.

Here's a tip to begin the whole process correctly: Whenever you get up to speak, before you even get out of your chair to come to the front of the room, know which person with whom you're going to begin speaking. Decide whom you're going to start your presentation with before you get up, and stick with that person through your opening line. Otherwise, you're going to start off on the wrong foot; you're going to start scanning around for those "friendly faces". Choose ahead of time the person with whom you're going to begin, and start talking by looking at that one person and letting it flow.

Let's be clear — one thing you definitely don't want to do is to look for and speak to only a few "friendly faces". You may have run across that bit of advice before, but be forewarned: that advice might work well for the few faces, but what about all the other less than friendly mugs? How do you suppose they feel when they notice that you are engaging other people but not them? Do you suppose it might get them thinking about something other than your message? Do you want only a few people buying into what you're saying, or the whole group?

Your job is to look at *everyone* in the audience - at least from their perspective. Everyone in the room needs to leave feeling that you took the time to personally engage them as individuals. If you've been to a speech or a presentation by someone with *The Skills*, you have no doubt noticed that they did this. In fact, have you ever been to a large event with perhaps hundreds (or even thousands) of people and come away feeling that, throughout the program, the speaker kept coming back to you? That for some reason the speaker picked you out personally for special notice, and repeatedly?

This is perhaps the most powerful advantage you will have with *The Skills*, but it's also the easiest to acquire, because it happens all by itself! One great thing about *The Skills* is that they are what software designers would call infinitely scalable. That is, the larger the crowd, the better they work for you, but you don't work any harder. You engage in exactly the same behaviors with twelve people as you do with twelve hundred!

A Parallax Universe

The job of looking at everyone in the audience is actually easier done than said. Thanks to the ways our eyes are built, from distances as short as ten feet, a phenomenon known as *parallax* kicks in, and for the very same reason we see railroad tracks converge in the distance, our eyes see the other person's eyes converging on ours even when they might be pointed a few feet away.

Speakers with *The Skills* are always only looking directly at one person at a time. But from a short distance, and increasingly with greater distance, people sitting around the person to whom the speaker is actually looking believe the speaker is looking directly at *them*. So from, say, fifteen feet away, the four people around the one person you're looking at will feel the benefits of your attention and feel that you are engaging them as individuals. From thirty feet, twelve people around your target will swear you've singled them out for attention! Your circle of influence keeps getting larger and larger, but you're just doing the exact same thing you'd do in a small conference room.

In our classes we enjoy asking if anyone has ever been to a concert where they felt the singer sang directly to them, and we inevitably get at least one response of, *"Yes, but how did you know?"* Rock stars know how to create and keep fans, and this skill is a big tool in their box.

Focused Attention

When you lock on one person, everything else kind of fades away. You focus all of your attention on that one person and nothing else. For the moment, your entire universe is composed of the one person to whom you are directing your one thought. And when you do that, for those two to nine seconds or so, your brain doesn't have to make new threat calculations. It's free to direct its energy into developing and delivering the thought.

Just as when you work from a nice, clean desk, or when you're given just one task to do, by talking to only one person at a time, it creates a nice, strong point of focus. All of your attention can be given to this one moment, so that nothing else going on is affecting your brain. Focusing on one person creates an environment that helps you focus on one thought — the thought that you're delivering to that one person.

You're also able to pace yourself. When you learn how to pause - when you learn how to say what you have to say and then stop talking for a moment and move on to the next person before you begin speaking - you create a smooth pace that the audience can follow, and also one that doesn't foul you up.

When you present, adrenaline courses through your veins, your metabolism is raised, and all of your processes, including thinking, speed up. Consequently, your perception of time slows down. Thus, you tend to speak much more quickly than you perceive. And unfortunately with your somewhat diminished cognitive ability, it's sometimes possible for your mouth to overrun your brain. You push the words out so fast that your brain is not able to replenish the queue quickly enough and you find yourself with nothing to say.

This of course simply causes more anxiety and cranks up the whole fear juice thing even more. The more we get cranked up, the more time slows down. That's one of the reasons most people don't pause. In your slow-motion state, you believe your pauses to be much longer than what your audience hears. But when you've been speaking non-stop for some time, and you suddenly find yourself, at least temporarily with nothing to say, your pause is much more noticeable. By working pauses into your speech from the very beginning, you're able to establish a pace that seems natural to the audience, and will actually mask any moment when you might not be able to think of what to say.

First on My Mind

Perhaps the process that skews the overall impact of a presentation most is the conscious tracking of word choice and flow. Unless trained otherwise – as you will be by the end of this chapter - you might believe that the primary focus of any presenter should be the next thing he or she is about to say. In fact, most speakers are constantly forming the next word group in their heads, even while spouting their current string. The trouble is, when the oratorical lens is focused directly upon a set of words, just having that next set ready is never really good enough.

For example, what if, upon uttering the doctored phraseology, you realize your word choices still weren't sufficient enough to clearly articulate your desired message? Well at that point, the average speaker will slap on another prepositional phrase or subordinate clause in an effort to make her words parse. But if *that* impromptu addition proves to be no more than an artificial appendage, it is essential to have even *more* words ready, just in case.

You see where this is going? Almost all speakers work from a cue of thoughts, stacked six, eight, even ten high. As their words spill out, the next thought falls down in the cue awaiting escape, and so on and so forth. This lineup of words is always the most important thought on a speaker's mind; God help you if you reached for those words one time and they weren't there! Of course, just to make the process more confusing, the speaker is also trying to manage this automatic Pez Dispenser of verbiage while distributing the flow of words to a new customer every second. Every *second*!

Think this process might have an effect on the quality of the product emerging from the speaker's mouth?

The Alternative

Consider this: Things change for the better really quickly when, rather than taxing your mind with what to say next, you stop and pause. If the pause is foremost in your list of priorities, you're always working toward the next pause. And if you know you have to take a break after every thought, then the only words you'll ever have to manage are those very few it takes to fill the space between the last pause taken and the next one coming up!

Instead of the six, eight or ten groups of words competing for position in your cue, you're thinking about...oh, that's right...only one! One group of words at a time – perhaps not even a complete sentence – all while knowing that in a few seconds you'll have a moment (the pause) to come up with the next single group. That's not working very hard. That's uni-tasking.

And when you think about it, it's the same process you use when you engage in polite conversation. Nothing is pre-planned. You utter one thought and then you shut up [pause] and let the other person speak, and then it's back to you.

Learning to not work hard, as you can see, is a huge part of *The Skills*.

Sending the Proper Signals

When you speak to individuals in the group rather than to an amorphous blob, you send a very strong signal that you don't have a problem looking somebody in the eye. When you can talk to audience members and tell them how great your product is, or how you're going to save them so much money, how you're going to save them time, how you're going to put them ahead of the competition, how you're going to make their life easier; when you can say all that, and look somebody in the eye as you say it, you send a signal.

The signal, both consciously and subconsciously, tells them you have nothing to hide. They can trust you, and put credence in what you tell them. Your audience can believe what you're saying, because you look them in the eye.

This approach works for a speech or presentation on any topic, by any type of organization. The approach becomes *essential* for anyone in the business of selling trust. If your industry is one built on the client's needing to have absolute faith in the veracity of your words (financial planning, insurance, real estate investment, etc.), then you are wasting a lot of time – and prospects – if you try to convince them with Aerosol Eyes.

Finally, when you can speak to the individuals in an audience, you create a whole new group dynamic. When you engage them one on one, everyone knows that they are not just part of a blob where they're never going to be "called on" or ever taken to task. Now you severely alter their expectations, and thus their reactions.

When audience members know that although you might not be talking to them just now, but eventually you're going to come back around and speak directly to them; when they realize that they're part of a one-on-one event, they find that their role in the process changes too.

> **Essential point:** Lock, Talk and Pause creates a *bond* with the audience where the members, instead of being somewhat removed *observers* of someone's performing into the ether, now become *participants* in an event.

You create a bond with the audience that never existed before, a bond that is simply not possible to establish when you're spraying the audience with your vision and words in a different direction every second. Now, people actually listen to what you're saying, because they *can*. Instead of wondering when you're going to stop speaking so that their fragile little brains can get a rest, they're actually waiting for your next words. People are wondering when you're going to come around and talk to them again. They know that they are indeed part of what's going on, and not just this once, twice, thrice removed observer. You can imagine the difference in the impact of your message. And that's the key. Everything changes when you Lock, Talk, and Pause.

Points to Remember

- Lock, Talk & Pause reduces your brain's need to complete new threat calculations, thus reducing the call for adrenaline, and restoring cognitive ability.
- Lock eyes. Talk to one person through the completion of a thought. Pause before engaging the next person.
- Instead of trying to manage a cue of endless word tracks, make the next pause your constant priority. That way, you can concentrate on only the *very* next thing you're going to say, and not on the next and the next and the next...
- Before you begin your presentation, choose the first person with whom you will lock eyes.
- With ever larger groups, those sitting near your target "eyes" will perceive you are looking directly at them.

Suggested Exercises

You can practice the Lock, Talk & Pause method in the privacy of your home. To do that, you will need the text of the famous speech found in Appendix A at the end of this book.

Also, you will need to download and print:

www.publicspeakingskills.com/cato/Eyes.pdf

If you wish to have control over font size, you can download the speech at this page, too:

www.publicspeakingskills.com/cato/Dream.pdf

The *Eyes* file is a set of faces that you will assemble on chairs around your dining room table, or in any room here you can simulate actually speaking to real people. The more realistic you can make the setting, the better. Just fold the pages in half and drape them over the chair backs. If you don't have a printer, draw a pair of eyes on four or more pieces of 8½ x 11 inch paper, folded width-wise.

The *I Have A Dream* file is the beginning of the famous speech by Martin Luther King, who moved millions around the world with his mastery of *The Skills*.

1. Deliver this short speech to your paper audience. Give one concept at a time to a different set of eyes.

   Repeat the exercise at least six times, or as many times as necessary until you know you're doing it right. The first three times you try it, just try getting comfortable with the words. Take a break. For the next three times, because you'll know the material better, concentrate on making sure you don't deliver each line until you have found a set of eyeballs to receive it. Remember, you must first acquire the target before you pull the trigger.

   After that, repeat as many times as you feel is necessary to comfortably achieve what we call 'hang time'. Hang time is the amount of time you hang in with your listener after the last words have left your mouth. This should be roughly the time it would take to say, *"Do you know what I mean?"* or *"Did you hear what I said?"* You don't say those things out loud, of course. But you might infer them with your eyes.

2. After you feel you have Lock, Talk, and Pause down cold, and you've become comfortable with your newfound friends (the Eyes), now it's time to use *The Skills* with material of your own. Try this one: Run your 'group' through a process with which you're very familiar. For instance, all the steps it takes to bake an apple pie from scratch. Or how to approach, plan and execute a fairway shot. Or how to setup a fan page on facebook. Anything that lends itself to a step-by-step set of instructions.

   Don't spend a lot of time preparing here. The process is more important than the content, and you'll want to learn to apply *The Skills* when asked to speak impromptu (more on this later). Experiment with not trying to think about what you're going to say until just before you deliver it. In other words, practice NOT thinking about anything other than the *very next* thought you're about to share.

3. Throughout the next week, force yourself to practice your new skills every time you are speaking to someone. Obviously, the more opportunities you find to speak to a group of people the better. Understand that when you first talk to real people this way, it may feel a little uncomfortable because humans are not always comfortable when changing old behaviors.

   For the first week or so, you are going to have to concentrate on Lock, Talk & Pause every time you speak. The good news is because this new behavior requires significantly less energy than the old way, soon enough you will start doing it without thinking, because your brain and body will find it easy to slip into a "lazy" new habit!

The more you concentrate on implementing the new behaviors, the quicker they will become your second nature.

> *"Truth, like gold, is to be obtained not by its growth, but by washing away from it all that is not gold."*
>
> - Leo Tolstoy

Chapter 4:
The Power of the Pause

If you were studious in your executions of the exercises in chapter 3, you should now feel at ease with maintaining constant eye-contact with those to whom you speak. You should also know what it's like to speak to a single person through the end of one thought before moving on to the next person. If you haven't practiced the exercises, both with the sample speech and in your daily routines, we strongly suggest you do so before continuing with this chapter.

In our classes, participants work through a number of exercises and quickly agree that it's much more comforting to present your message to one person at a time. You're no longer cranking up your whole inner reaction system and are able to settle down and be more comfortable. The more comfortable you feel, the more comfortable the audience feels, because they empathize with you. And the more comfortable they are, the more likely they are to absorb your message.

The *"Lock, Talk"* parts of the program are not too difficult to learn. As we alluded to before, the most difficult part to master is *"& Pause"*. Yet, as we'll examine in this chapter, it is the most important component of the process of speaking well. Speakers who have *The Skills* have learned to embrace the pause.

But why is the pause so important?

The pause is important for three reasons:

1. *It allows your audience to hear what you just said*

2. *It prepares them to hear what you're about to say next*

3. *It gives you the time to prepare your next thought*

Textbook vs. Newspaper

It's important to understand that the pause in speech is equivalent to the paragraph in the written word. When you end one paragraph and begin a new one, you are moving to a new thought or a new concept. It works the same way in speech.

Consider a science textbook (organic chemistry, anyone?) that carries page after page of text without a single break. Many of us didn't make it through organic chemistry in college, because when we opened up the textbook, we flipped through a few pages and just said,

"No way!" You saw an unending stream of words and decided that your brain was simply not equipped to take in all that stuff.

That's exactly how your listeners feel when you speak without pausing. You don't see them slam the book shut on you, but they do silently shut out much of what you say, choosing to wait for the handout. They still smile and nod when you look at them, but they're not hearing you. They can't hear you, because *people start listening only when you stop talking*.

Now compare the chemistry textbook to a newspaper. Until you pick one up and count, many people aren't aware that the average newspaper paragraph contains only two sentences (in *USA Today*, sometimes less than one!). Why? Because newspapers are in the same business as you are when delivering a presentation. Newspapers deliver new information to people quickly, and then move on.

Newspaper editors know they have one shot to give it to you, because most people don't hold on to newspapers. They're not used as reference material. You read them one time and toss them on your way off the train.

So the process of getting new information to people quickly involves being able to parcel it out into bite-size morsels that the brain can digest. The paragraph is key to that. Think about the physical structure of a paragraph. You read across the column: one sentence, two sentences, and then get a nice little piece of whitespace. That white space is brain rest. And before you're asked to take in more information, you get a little indent - a bit more white space. More brain rest. That's what a paragraph is all about.

Speaking in Paragraphs

> *"The right word may be effective, but no word was ever as effective as a rightly timed pause".*
>
> Mark Twain

Mark Twain understood that people only start listening when you stop talking.

He also understood that the pause in speech works exactly the same way. In order to get your audience to really take in what you have to say, you've got to stop talking and give their brains a rest. Frequently. Stop talking long enough for them to digest that last thing you said, get a picture of it, and try to put it into a context that they understand before you move on to the next thing you're going to say.

> **Essential Point:** The pause is absolutely the most important part of the process of speaking. Every great speaker knows this, and the sooner you learn to embrace the pause the sooner people will think of you as a great speaker, too.

Most people think speaking is all about the content. But time can go on quite nicely even when not filled with your words! As you listen to the speakers in the video links later in this chapter, you will appreciate why those with *The Skills* not only embrace the pause, they strive to master it.

Mastering the Pause

When you learn to pause, you establish the pace from the beginning of your talk. In the first crucial 30 seconds, you telegraph to your audience that the information is going to be coming at them at a pace that they can handle. You let them know right up front that you will be delivering your story in the form of a newspaper — not a textbook.

So to put the process all together:

Find one person, give one thought, and take one pause.

Make your pause long enough for them to digest the last thing you said, reference it and catalog it, before you ask them to open up to new information. Keep in mind this doesn't have to be a long period of time. Depending on the volume of information you just imparted, it may be a half-second, a second, or maybe two. The more important or salient the point, the longer the pause. But throughout your presentation, the process is the same:

One person, one thought, one pause.

When you engage these behaviors, you will find your relationship with the audience changes in many ways. Not only does the group dynamic change, but also the type of feedback you get from the group. In many cases, you'll find people in the audience who've been through lifetimes of presentations and never felt engaged at that same level.

When you master *Lock, Talk,* & (especially) *Pause,* you will find people coming up to you at the end of the meeting or presentation and say things such as, *"You know, Jane, I've heard this information before, but nobody's ever explained it in quite the same way. Somehow, you made it all understandable"*. Or, *"You really helped me understand. This was a great presentation"*. You gave them the ability to actually hear what you said.

This type of positive feedback will reinforce your desire to hone *The Skills* every time you speak. And understand this: you will get a little better every time you do. In fact, speaking well is a lifelong process — one that continues to improve as long as you do it.

Learning from the Grand Masters

When asked to name the greatest public speakers in our time, many of us think of Martin Luther King, John F. Kennedy, Ronald Reagan, or Bill Clinton. [Barack Obama is sometimes included in the list, but though he is a great student of *The Skills*, he's still got some work to do. People with *The Skills* execute them every time, not just in prepared environments.]

To be fair, there are also some great female speakers out there, but their politics often clouds the public's perception of their speaking ability. Governor Sarah Palin will be a truly great speaker when she learns to pause. Carly Fiorina and Elisabeth Hasselbeck are both captivating to listen to, and should be role models for female speakers everywhere, regardless of their leanings.

Let's take a look at some of these Grand Masters.

President Clinton can attribute much of his success to his ability to speak well. But he wasn't always a great speaker; this was something he needed to learn to become President. One problem he had to tackle was his habit of pointing at his audience. People feel uncomfortable when pointed at, and we know how important it is for audience members to feel comfortable. His handlers never could get him to break the gesture completely, so instead they convinced him to crank that first finger back into his hand and lock it down with his thumb.

Who can forget the famous clip of President Clinton with his fist moving up and down, thumb pointed outward as it held a firm grip on his finger, declaring to the assembled press, *"I did not have relations with that woman, that Monica Lewinsky..."*

But, more importantly, Clinton needed to master The Pause. And he has done so with great success. There's no speaker today who knows more about how to get a message across by saying a few words and then pausing to let them sink in. In fact, Bill Clinton probably says fewer words between pauses than any other politician.

When you listen to Clinton speak, you find yourself not only hearing what he just said, but also anticipating his next words. And that is the second reason the pause is so vital. When you fill your stream of thoughts with abundant opportunities for your audience to rest, you will find their actually waiting to hear your next words. With most speakers, audiences can't wait for them to stop so that their brains can get a little rest. But when you pause frequently, audiences actually wait in anticipation for your next words. They are primed to listen, they want to hear more, and the impact of your words is much greater.

Bill Clinton learned *The Skills* by listening to his hero — John F. Kennedy. Both speakers consider the needs of the listener as they talk. They give everyone all the time they need to absorb what they say and to form a clear picture of the words before asking them to take in new information.

The Speeches

If you have access to the Internet, copy the links below and listen to two great examples of Masters of the Pause. Listen to them several times. But the first time through, just watch and listen. Make no attempt to analyze anything, but rather listen for how easy it is to follow their thoughts.

President Bill Clinton gives his 1997 inaugural address:

    www.publicspeakingskills.com/cato/Clinton.wmv

President John F. Kennedy speaks to the graduating class of American University in 1963:

    www.publicspeakingskills.com/cato/Kennedy.wmv

Replay the Clinton speech. This time, close your eyes and listen. Count the number of words he delivers between pauses — you're looking for an average. What did you find? Does it surprise you? How does Clinton's average compare to yours?

It's common to believe that some people are born with the talent to speak well and, therefore, no amount of training or practicing is going to transform you into a great speaker. And while it's true that both Kennedy and Clinton have another important characteristic — charisma — it's essential to remember that their skill at speaking was not a birthright.

We repeat: Bill Clinton was not always a great speaker. He was guilty of several bad practices, one being common to the political class: Clinton actually thought people wanted to hear elected officials go on at the mouth for one, two, or even three hours. He did exactly that as governor of Arkansas. And yet you rarely hear someone say, *"That was a great presentation — I only wished he would have droned on for another hour or so"*.

The Passing of the Torch

Replay the Kennedy speech, and perform the same exercise. Close your eyes and count the number of words Kennedy says between pauses and you will see where Bill Clinton found his style. Clinton's speaking style is simply a modernized version of Kennedy's.

JFK was one of the most influential speakers of the 20th century because he introduced the "humanistic" style of public speaking. Prior to Kennedy's showing the world the power of an authoritarian speaking to his "subjects" on equal terms, we had the "oratory" style, best exemplified by Winston Churchill. Churchill spoke to us from on high. Kennedy brought speech down to the level of the common man, and people loved him for it.

We are not suggesting that every time you give a speech or deliver a presentation you should speak as if you were the president of your country. We show you Kennedy and Clinton because they exemplify how powerful the *Pause* can be to the art of persuasion. Few people will ever use as many pauses when they present as these and other Masters of *The Skills*. But most people won't be speaking often to audiences of 10,000 or more either.

If you are not able to listen to the speeches, here's help. In his speech President Clinton averages 4.7 words between pauses. Sometimes, though rarely, he'll say as many as 9 or 10 words in a row; but at least a third of the time he says 3 words, pauses, then 3 more, then a pause, then 3 more. As you can imagine, it's not very difficult to actually hear and remember what he says when he parcels it out in 3-word morsels.

Listen to Kennedy closely and you'll notice that on more than one occasion he actually says just one word and then pauses. Most of his sentences have as many pauses as word groups.

Again, we bring these Masters of The Pause to your attention not to suggest you mimic them every time you speak, but to draw attention to the fact that there's likely quite a difference between your average word count between pauses and theirs. Our internal research has shown that the average business speaker strings together 20 to 25 words between pauses, if they pause at all. We want you to listen to the Masters and work towards making your speeches or presentations as memorable as theirs, with the understanding of how deeply pausing plays to that theme.

An Inconvenient Speaker

If you doubt that Bill Clinton's ability to embrace the pause may have been responsible for his being elected, take a look at the other side. A great example of somebody who didn't until recently have a *clue* about the pause is Al Gore. Do you think of Al Gore as being a great speaker? Do you think there might be a relationship between his speaking ability and the fact that he couldn't maintain Clinton's dynasty?

When Al Gore delivered his acceptance speech for the presidential nomination at the 2000 Democratic convention, he had a laundry list of ideas that he thought was very important to get out. He had 45 minutes in which to deliver them.

During the first 20 minutes of his speech, people in the audience would hear things that they liked and, quite naturally, applaud. At least they tried to applaud. [Mr. Gore would describe his relationship with the audience as "complicated".] But instead of pausing and bathing in the glow for a moment or two, Mr. Gore would hold up his hands to silence them and just kept on speaking. This went on for 25 minutes — the audience applauded, and he wouldn't stop speaking. The audience soon became uncomfortable because they were applauding over him.

The applause then became more sporadic and eventually stopped altogether. And so for the last 20 minutes of the speech, he continued to speak, and nobody applauded at all. He spoke for 20 minutes straight. Not a single break.

If you were to have given a pop quiz to the audience and asked them how many of his ideas for America they could remember, you probably would have found no person remembering more than three. Mr. Gore focused only on the content of his speech, not his audience's ability to take it all in. Although he had served eight years under The Master of The Pause, it never occurred to the Inventor of the Internet to study just what made his boss so successful.

Years later, before filming *An Inconvenient Truth*, Al Gore sought and received professional presentation skills training, and he has a somewhat better grasp on the process than when he ran for president in 2000. In fact, in a May 2007 article in *The New York Times*, Gore was asked if he had any regrets about how he ran the campaign. The reporter was hoping to get him to say something related to the legal process, but instead Gore replied, *"If I had had the presentation skills I've since learned, I think I'd be in my second term as president"*.

Points to Remember

- The pause is the heart of all great speech.
- The pause has three benefits: it allows your audience to hear what you said; it prepares them to hear what you are going to say next, and it gives you time to prepare your next thought.
- The pause in speech is equal to the paragraph break in print.
- Pausing every few words is *not* too frequent. You want to strive for, at the very least, pausing at the end of a complete thought.

Suggested Exercises

These exercises require a bit of vigilance on your part to have the desired effect. You must practice them *at every opportunity* this week.

1. Replay both the Clinton and the Kennedy videos until you can hear them in your head at will. You may want to play each a couple of times a day, every day. The objective is to fully appreciate how each of these Masters uses time and silence for maximum effect. Know that pausing after only two, three or four words is not only acceptable, but also can be extremely powerful. Know, too, that lack of pausing leads to lack of attention and lack of audience comprehension.

2. Download Bill Clinton's '97 Inaugural Address from:

    www.publicspeakingskills.com/cato/Inaugural.pdf

3. Reconstruct your private audience of "Eyes" from the previous chapter, and give the speech as it is broken out. Give only one line of the presentation to each pair of eyes and then move on. Use the time it takes to read the printout for your next line as your pause. Note that some lines run to 10 words, while others are as few as one. Get a feel for what it sounds like when you yourself pause for approximately as long as Clinton does.

4. When you speak to anyone this week, whether groups or individuals, employ this technique: Speak in one complete thought, and then take a full, conscious breath. It need not be deep or obvious — just a normal inhale and exhale. Then say your next thought. Repeat until done. If speaking to a group, be sure to give each next thought to a new person.

5. Observe your audience's response. If a listener jumps in with her own thought during your pause, accept it and wait until your next turn. Unless conveying bad news, do not hesitate to smile — smiling defuses threatening signals that prolonged direct eye contact may convey. Be sure to practice this exercise at least once a day; your goal is getting to a point where you know to pause (and breathe) between thoughts.

6. Lest you think this style is strictly American in nature, take a look at the most successful politician, in terms of longevity, in the free world post World War II:

    www.publicspeakingskills.com/cato/TonyBlaire.wmv

Chapter 5:
Putting Passion in Your Pitch

The good news and the bad news about passion is this: with the proper display of passion, you could break almost all the 'rules' about proper *delivery* and still deliver an effective speech. Some great speakers do occasionally break the rules, but they get away with it because they wrap you up so tightly in their passion that you don't notice. Think Tony Robbins.

Peggy Noonan, the WSJ columnist and former speech writer for President Reagan, is fond of saying, referring to audiences, *"They won't care how much you know, until they know how much you care"*. With the easy accessibility to vast amounts of information today, there are many people who know a great deal. But knowledge matters very little if you can't convey what you know with a level of passion that drives people to sit up and listen. After all, it's not likely that anybody in the audience is going to care more about your topic than you do, so to ensure that audiences come away interested and motivated to learn more, it's incumbent upon you, the speaker, to stretch to the point of almost going over the top with passion and enthusiasm for your topic.

So how exactly do you convey passion?

Gestures

An important thing to know about gestures is how they affect the energy equation of your presentation. Every time you move the muscles in your upper body it burns some of your excess energy. In a modern-world, one-against-many environment, it's not healthy for your career or your freedom if you choose to fight your audience or flee the scene.

So what do you do with that pent up energy? You move your arms and hands in concert with the words coming out your mouth. You paint pictures of the words or the action you're describing. We say "in concert" because these movements should be fluid and work harmoniously with your message. Using inappropriate or rigid movements can distract from the message rather than add to it.

And we define gesturing as moving the muscles of your *upper* body, because with the possible exception of Elvis Presley, very few of us can add to the presentation with movement of the lower body.

Most new speakers don't gesture at all. Or their gestures are so reserved that they fail to either burn off energy or signal enthusiasm. You need to put enough energy into your gestures to burn calories and to let your audiences know that you care enough about your topic to actually get physical about it.

As easy as it is to define distracting gestures and nuances, it is also fairly easy to adopt the practices that can define you as a professional presenter. In this chapter, we'll work on the basics of maximizing your impact on the audience by getting physical .

The Neutral Position

Begin by balancing your stance, feet shoulder width apart. Keep your arms at your sides — not in your pockets, or fiddling with your clothes. This is called the "neutral position". In the neutral position, your hands are not locked together either in front of you or behind you. The trouble with hands is that they often act like electro-magnets – as soon as they come into proximity to each other they lock together and are almost impossible to pull apart.

From the neutral position, use your hands to gesture when appropriate, and then return to neutral between gestures. Gesture from the shoulders, not the elbows. Use your hands to describe and emphasize.

When you gesture from the neutral position, your gestures become more emphatic. If everything comes from the middle magnet position it looks like you are stuck in a phone booth. Granted, dropping your hands to your side is not as easy as it sounds. With most people the hands immediately come back together like magnets, or start grabbing things like your clothing, face or hair. Sometimes they'll even jump into your pockets.

If you are talking about an increase in sales, show us by raising your arm. If you mention something about reducing costs, show us with a downward motion. In other words, be sure you don't use the same gesture for an increase as you did for a decrease.

> **Essential Point:** Gesturing actually helps you think. It reduces the cognitive load by transferring part of the descriptive process from your brain to your body. Have you ever noticed someone talking on the phone and gesturing with the other hand - even though the person on the other end can't see his gestures? Gesturing helps you relax and find the correct dialogue. And, you have something to do with your arms!

Lecterns

Most people refer to the lectern as a podium even though the podium (from the Greek "pod" for feet) is actually the platform upon which the lectern stands. Lecterns are a problem for both the speaker and the audience. It's rare to see a speaker behind a lectern whose hands aren't white-knuckled and riveted to the edges as if he were being hit with a 10,000 volt current.

If your speaking venue is equipped with a lectern, one of the most effective things you can do is say your opening words from behind it, and then just walk out and expose yourself to the audience. Lecterns go back to the oratory era of Churchill and FDR. They worked to help separate the speaker from the audience. And that's exactly what a lectern does. They provide a visible, physical barrier between you and the audience when you really ought to be trying to engage and bond with.

Less is More

In order to display passion, you can't be a prisoner of your slides – you can't let them steal the audience's attention and leave you as a bit player in the process. As you'll learn in Chapter 6, if you're delivering an onscreen presentation, you need to limit the amount of data thrown onto the screen at any one time. When it comes to words, a properly designed presentation never has any more than the absolute fewest words it takes to clue the audience where you're going, and to cue you to speak from your own internal knowledge base.

Having *The Skills* also means knowing how to balance the amount of information you try to impart to the audience at any given time. By lightening the load of information to deliver, presenters with *The Skills* find themselves able to expend their energy in directed, meaningful output that audiences read as true passion.

You must understand that content is by far *not* the most important aspect of the presentation process. Most presenters put way too much content into their presentations in an effort to impress the audience with the breadth and depth of their knowledge. Yet no matter how important your content might be, if you don't both look good (confident & comfortable) and sound good (with the solid timbre of sincerity and expertise in your voice), nobody will take what you say seriously enough for you to have an impact. Concentrating on the content too often results in losing the big picture. People need to hear and see how much you care about what you say. They need to feel your passion for the subject.

Volume

Many people can double and even triple their volume, and still not deliver at the level they should. If 10 is glaringly loud music, and 1 is virtually inaudible, you need to be at about a 7 or 8 when presenting to a large group. (For a small group, you still want at least a 6.)

Listening is hard work. Your job is to make yourself easy to be heard. Think how often you've been tempted to tune-out during a boring presentation, or really have to work to remain awake.

Raising your inflection and volume will grab the audiences' attention instantly. It will also help you let more steam out of the pot, make you feel more comfortable, and exude higher levels of confidence. Just raising your voice alone, however, is not enough.

You also need to use variety in your voice. Change the variation in length of the sentences, the loudness, the tone, and the pace. Use different sentence types like assertions, questions, and exclamations. Use inflections to signal words of importance. And by all means, remember to pause!

Inflection

I didn't say I want to date her.

I **didn't** say I want to date her.

I didn't **say** I want to date her.

I didn't say **I** want to date her.

I didn't say I **want** to date her.

I didn't say I want to **date** her.

I didn't say I want to date **her**.

We can say the same things, use the exact same words, and relate entirely different ideas based on where we place our inflection. Inflection means variance in the pitch and the tone of the voice. It's simply more interesting to listen to someone who speaks with varying degrees of speed and intonation than to someone who has either a loud barrage of dialogue or a non-stop, low volume monotone.

When describing voice inflection it is helpful to think topography. For example, someone with very little voice inflection is like the plains of Kansas. Some voice inflection might be similar to the hills of Santa Barbara or Pennsylvania, while lots of inflection — what you want to use — would be like The Rocky Mountains.

One of the easiest ways to show passion is to change your inflection, accompanied by raising the volume on words or phrases you feel strongly about.

How NOT to speak at Carnegie Hall

After "look at everyone in the audience", the next most commonly heard bit of advice given to speakers is "practice, practice, practice". Many presenters think the key to overcoming nervousness and appearing confident is to know their word tracks cold. In other words, memorize a script.

Here's the problem with scripts: if you think that speaking is about following a script, about saying a set of preset words, you must understand that speaking from a script tends to flatten out your delivery. Unless you're a trained actor, you lose the ability to put natural inflection into your words, and as we have seen, inflection can often completely change the meaning of what it is you are trying to say. It's very difficult to use a lot of tone and inflection if you're trying to deliver a predetermined set of words.

Have you ever listened to your favorite radio DJ, whose natural personality comes out when he or she is speaking spontaneously, but who sounds boring, stilted, silly, or just plain phony when forced to read an ad from a script? These people are trained in the vocal arts, yet most *sound* scripted when they're not allowed to speak freely. Imagine how audiences must feel when an untrained person spouts from a memorized script?

Essential Point: Rather than practice, practice, practice, people with *The Skills* know the key is to prepare, prepare, prepare.

Prepare, Prepare, Prepare

Before your next presentation, learn everything you can (or have time to) about your topic. Talk to colleagues who are also knowledgeable about the subject. Read as much as you can. Search the Internet. If you're lucky, you might even find some video, which will stick in your mind more than words.

Then go back and look at your slides.

Can you speak for three to five minutes on each of your bullet points? If you can't, consider tossing your short points out. If you can, then you know that if you try to speak for only one or two minutes each, you'll never run out of things to say before clicking your mouse and moving on.

Permission to Not Care

In the movie, *The Fugitive*, Lieutenant Gerard catches up with Dr. Kimball near the outlet of a high dam. Gerard had been chasing Kimball not as a suspect in a crime (the murder of Kimball's wife), but as fugitive from justice. With seemingly no where to go, and Gerard's gun trained on him, Kimball still hesitates to surrender. Looking Gerard straight in the eye, Kimball shouts,

"I didn't kill my wife!"

Lt. Gerard, staring back at his captured prey, replies,

"I don't care!"

Gerard's job was to apprehend a fugitive, regardless of his guilt or innocence as a murderer.

Sometimes as a presenter you have to learn to accept that as long as you are performing by the rules, you can't necessarily care about how you are being received by every member of the audience.

In other words, one thing that should never be a source of discomfort for you is a particular audience member's response to your engagement at any one time.

When you employ the discipline of picking your target and looking him in the eyes, completing your thought and then pausing before finding your next target, there will be times when your new target has his head down or is otherwise not returning your engagement. Of course, once the audience realizes that you are actually engaging them as individuals, that will happen much less often. But when it does happen, you have to learn not to care.

After you have picked your target, deliver your message regardless of whether the person is looking back. Do not shift from one person to the next to find another target. It's okay. Give yourself permission to not care. Remember that those people seated near your chosen person have already locked in on you and will feel slighted if you look away.

Part of the anxiety speakers feel is based on their ongoing assessment of what the audience is thinking about them. The brain is always going to make a worst-case assessment because it needs to err on the side of caution. It's going to think the worst, and determine that there's a threat.

In the absence of any totally proactive — *oh, yes, you're great, I love you* — response, your brain will think all sorts of bad things. Your brain is looking for threats all the time, and so that's what it finds.

When you turn to somebody who is asleep or has his head down, you're likely to think your speech is boring. In reality, that person may have had a rough night. You don't know what that person is experiencing. There are unlimited reasons why that person might not be giving you totally positive feedback. Because the chances that YOU are the problem are slight, you have to learn to simply not care and carry on for the 99% of the audience that is with you.

Be Yourself

People with a true command of *The Skills* know that a large part of engaging the audience is simply being *you*. Most presenters often think that once they get up to speak, they need to take on an entirely new persona.

People do not come to a presentation to hear what you have to say. They don't come to be impressed by your knowledge base. There are other less troublesome ways for them to acquire information. They are actually there for your humanness. They want to see and hear information delivered by a human. They're human. They know what it's like. They want to see what *value* you can add to the information they could otherwise get from a handout (and read on their own time).

The more spontaneous you can be, the less "practiced" you seem, the more likely you will come across as the genuine person you are, and the more impact you will have on your audience. And when you learn to forget the fact that there are 5, 50 or 500 people out there, and you learn to speak to one (and only one) person at a time, you'll realize that public speaking is little different from having a conversation across a lunch table.

Once again: the system works because you're never speaking to a group of individuals, only to the individuals in the group.

Do you feel uncomfortable talking one-on-one to people? Most people don't. Similarly, when you have a discussion with somebody about what's going on at work, do you prepare for it for three or four hours ahead of time? Do you go to lunch with a coworker toting a written set of talking points and a practiced set of word tracks, or do you just let it flow?

You will become a master of *The Skills* only when you convince yourself that you must approach your presentation well prepared, but not necessarily well-practiced. You don't want to be practiced, because it's going to flatten out your delivery. Like your favorite disc jockey reading that scripted ad. It almost always comes out flat. A flat delivery has less passion. And it's passion that people come to hear and feel.

Smile

When all else fails, smile.

If you can't do any of the things you've learned in this book so far, learn to smile. Great communicators know how effective smiling can be. People are hard-wired from birth to be receptive to a smile — and thus more receptive to your message when you do. Plus, smiles are contagious.

We conducted a presentation skills class some years back for The World Bank. The group was comprised of people from every continent except Antarctica. Now whenever we talk about the way we equate eye contact with veracity, we always preface it by saying, in *Western* cultures, we assign a lot of value to eye contact because we equate looking people in the eye with telling the truth. In this class, a woman from Kenya told us that in many cultures in Africa, a little bit of eye contact is a good thing. Too much eye contact is a bad thing.

She explained to the group that if you avoided eye contact when talking to somebody, they didn't trust you. If you held eye contact too long, they would kill you. Evidently, the way that you ameliorate the threat from sustained eye contact is by smiling. So if you want to talk to somebody, have eye contact, but for prolonged eye contact, it never hurts to do it with a smile. It disarms people. And when people are disarmed, they're more receptive to your message.

In Chapter 7 we explore at length the way the human brain processes different forms of incoming information differently. For now, accept the fact that speech is a form of information that our brains don't readily absorb. When we receive information in the form of speech or text or numbers or sequences, we don't just absorb them at face value — our brain first filters the information before it stores it or acts on it. There's always a wall; there's always a barrier going on in your audience's brain.

You can help overcome that barrier with a smile.

---

*"Knowing is not enough; we must apply.
Willing is not enough; we must do."*

- Goethe

Points to Remember

Congratulations! You have arrived at the end of the physical aspects of your presentation training. This is the beginning of your new life as a speaker that people will respect, admire, and perhaps even envy. If you have been true to yourself and practiced the exercises, you are well on your way to mastering *The Skills*. Mastery only comes with practice, however, and until the new behaviors become second nature to you, a process that depends on how often you get to use *The Skills*, you will have to put forth continued effort to make sure you're doing everything you need. Here's a review so far:

- *Lock* eyes on one person before you begin to speak.
- *Talk* to one, and only one, person at a time no matter how large the group.
- Instead of the next thing you're going to say being foremost on your mind, train yourself to accept that the most important thing must be your next *pause*.
- **Use the pause to compose your next thought.**
- Never try to compose anything more than your *very* next thought.
- People don't come to hear you speak — they come to hear your passion about your topic.
- To express your passion, use meaningful gestures, strong volume and interesting tone and inflection.
- At all times, be yourself.
- When all else fails, smile.

Suggested Exercises

1. You can have a lot of fun with this exercise, but you need at least one other person for your audience.

   - Download the MS PowerPoint® file:
     www.publicspeakingskills.com/cato/gestures.ppt
   - Each slide is a vignette of twelve lines of "script". For this particular exercise, we are using grammatically correct sentences (not something you would do in a real presentation)..
   - Running in SlideShow mode, click to bring up each line. When it appears on the screen, read it to yourself, then turn to face your audience. Deliver the entire line word-for-word, employing the gesture that the text implies. Don't be shy. Instead, see how far you can stretch. You won't know your true comfort zone unless you test and know your limits.

   After you have performed each slide at least twice, repeat as many times as you feel necessary to comfortably achieve what we call 'hang time'. Hang time is the amount of time you hang in with your listener after the last words have left your mouth. This should be roughly the time it would take to say, *"Do you know what I mean?"* or *"Did you hear what I said?"* You don't say those things, of course, but you might imply them with your eyes.

2. Using the same slides, demonstrate to yourself how you can come up with a complete thought in the moment. You can skip the gestures this time, or

continue to practice them if you're comfortable doing so while practicing a new skill. Your goal is to expand upon the vignette by adding your own content. As soon as the one line comes out of your mouth, follow it with a related line.

Example:

> The line we feed you is, *"So I rowed the boat to the middle of the lake..."*
>
> Instead of following with the line from the script, make one up on the spot. For example, *"...and I noticed I was quite a distance from the shore."*

Complete all three vignettes.

Over the next few weeks, concentrate on *Lock, Talk & Pause* every time you speak. The more you concentrate on implementing the new behaviors, the quicker they will become second nature to you.

Oh, and welcome to the club!

*It usually takes no more than three
weeks to prepare a good
impromptu speech"*

- Mark Twain

Part II:
Presentation Content

"Life consists not in holding good cards but in playing those you hold well."

- Josh Billings

Chapter 6:
Organizing Your Presentation

When organizing your presentation, remember that Less is More. Presentations generally have far too many details. Remember that it's about your audience, and about how much they can actually remember at the end of your talk. It's certainly not about the breadth and depth of your knowledge, even if the CEO is in the back of the room. Although we'd like to believe it, nobody will recall everything you say. Here's how to gather your thoughts, facts and persuasive efforts into a cohesive, yet concise presentation.

Give it a Name

Give your presentation a meaningful name. The key is to be very short and to the point. Describe the overall point of your presentation in a single sentence or "headline".

Start by writing a few full sentences to describe your overall theme. Edit out superfluous adjectives, and then see if you can combine the sentences into one. Then make that sentence a phrase. If you can't put all that into one headline you may have to simplify your idea.

Use a Structural Outline

To have maximum impact on the audience, first draft an outline of all of the content you intend to cover. The sample outline below is designed to get the audience's attention from the beginning, give them your information in the order in which it's easiest to catalog and retain, and then provide them with a reason to think about your presentation long after you're done.

You can structure virtually any presentation around this outline and know that you are maximizing the force of your message:

Start with a "Grabber"

    Problem/Opportunity

    Solution/Recommendation

        Support with Evidence

        Benefits to Audience

    Call to Action/Next Steps

End with a "Bang"

Getting off to the right start is absolutely critical. Notice that we do not include an Agenda or Company History in this outline. There is a reason for this as you will come to understand in Chapter 8. But for now, know that when your audience sees a slide containing an agenda or your company history, they slump back and prepare for another boring ride (i.e., *Oh, God, please! Been here, heard that.* Zzzzzzzzzzzz)

Grab their Attention

Quick: What's the name of the first slide you see in the vast majority of business presentations? That's right, the *AGENDA* slide. Even in a 15-minute presentation, we've seen the first couple minutes devoted to being told what we're going to hear in the next 12 or 13 - as if no one in the audience could hold their attention together for 15 minutes without knowing what they're going to hear next.

Of course, the Agenda slide is necessary to stick to that old adage, *"Tell them how you're gonna bore 'em, bore 'em, and then tell them how you bored 'em."*

Instead of starting with an agenda, arouse the audiences' curiosity with a shocking fact, a thought-provoking question, or anything that immediately engages them. We call it a "grabber". The audience is sizing you up in the first thirty seconds. They are thinking, *"Does this guy know what he's talking about? Is there a good reason for me to listen? What's in it for me?"* Use that first sentence, those first few words to make a major impact on your audience and take command of the room.

Film at 11

We've all heard the teasers, or "grabbers" that TV stations use to get your attention and make sure you tune in later. Local affiliate news stations having been doing this for decades. They entice you with something like,

"Coming up at 11: Doctors say exercise is BAD for you. Tune in tonight to find out more."

Or: *"FAA gets tough on airline safety. Death sentences for travelers? Story at 11."*

You don't ever want to incorporate dishonesty to get people to listen, but you need to whet the audience's appetite so they won't tune out. The key is to get the audience to think, *"Really? Tell me more!"* instead of, *"Oh, no. Been there. Heard that. Zzzzzzzzzzzzz."*

Research by Cox Communications, the large cable systems operator, shows that the typical TV surfer decides in 10 seconds or less whether or not to stay on a channel he's just selected. [Of course, science has shown that women use a remote to see what's on, while men use a remote to see what *else* is on.] Even worse, Cox further claims the average Web surfer, when using a search engine, allows only 2 seconds before deciding whether to stay on that page or go elsewhere. Audiences are much more forgiving with presenters. A recent study by UC Santa Cruz found that most audience members give the presenter 30 seconds to decide whether to keep listening or tune out.

Try to find a strong fact in your presentation that may

sound bizarre or impossible when taken out of context, but one you can support with actual facts during the presentation.

In the case of the TV news grabber, the story at 11(:20) was that a medical study had just concluded that men over the age of 85 who had suffered previous heart attacks and who engaged in marathons when the temperature was over 100 had a 50% chance of suffering another, often fatal heart attack! Hence, exercise can be *bad* for you!

A more serious (and true) example of a good grabber is the second one. If you do the math on the debacle that the FAA caused in 2008 when it chose to ground a fleet of 300 MD-80 jetliners, you find that by denying 400,000 passengers access to the absurdly high-level of airline safety, travelers were exposed to the increased dangers of *hundreds* of millions of miles of surface travel. Buried in those statistics (excuse the term) were likely numerous deaths from traffic accidents, as, according to the NHTSB there is a one fatality for every 15 million miles driven. *Death sentence for travelers?*

If the first 30 to 90 seconds of your presentation is devoted to covering the Agenda, and then moves on to a Company Overview followed by Revenue History, and the Organizational Chart, you can be sure you've already lost the vast majority of listeners. Instead, grab them from the beginning and never let go!

Problem or Opportunity

A well thought out "grabber" introduces the problem

that needs to be solved or the opportunity that needs to be embraced. Make sure the problem/opportunity is one that everyone can relate to and is expressed in a way everyone can understand.

Again, think in terms of headlines when developing your problem/opportunity. Don't get too verbose or wordy when considering your opening. An information data dump can overwhelm your audience and start them grabbing for their smart phones.

Sometimes presenting a problem connected to the consequences of no action can be powerful as well.

Solution / Recommendation

Next, present your solution or recommendation. This is where our outline differs from the typical structure we see in most business presentations. To ensure that your audience gets the most impact from your evidence, and to start the buy-in process as soon as possible, you must begin at the end. In other words, show them exactly where you're going to arrive before you start the journey.

When your audience knows your conclusion up front, they are able to put your evidence in context. When you introduce new evidence, you want them to think, *"I didn't know that. But given that piece of evidence, your conclusion makes a lot of sense!"* Without a framework into which you put the facts, it's more like, *"I didn't know that. Hmmm, I didn't know that, either. Hmmm, interesting. I wonder where he's going with all this…"*

Context is everything!

Although there are times in business where you must take a hard-line, direct approach, people like to come to conclusions on their own. By beginning at the end, you make it easier for people to convince themselves of the wisdom of your plan.

Be confident and enthusiastic about your solution or recommendation. You've set it up nicely with your "grabber" and presented it as a problem or opportunity. Here's your chance to share. Passion counts.

Next, you'll want to deliver evidence that unambiguously supports your solution or recommendation. It's often tempting to throw in facts or charts or other material that is *related* to your conclusion. But understand that anything you offer that doesn't directly aid their seeing a clear path to your destination will only work to counteract the impact of your really important evidence.

Nice-to-know information is good for filling time, but it more often dilutes the value and force of your *need*-to-know information, which is the only thing that you should ask your audience to attempt to retain.

Support with Evidence

Support that great solution/recommendation with evidence. Your audience, just like you, wants to see *proof*. There are four basic types of evidence:

   Personal
   Statistics
   Example
   Analogy

Consider your audience to help you to decide which type of evidence to choose.

Personal

Personal evidence involves you, first hand. Perhaps you were there or you saw something happen. This is probably the most interesting and powerful form of evidence. It also gives you extra credibility.

In a presentation, few forms of evidence are more captivating than someone talking about what happened to them personally. If a safety expert speaks about the statistics of airline safety, that's interesting; but imagine listening to an actual plane crash survivor. Which holds more interest?

The same goes for someone talking about a disease. Would you rather hear statistics involving millions, or the testimonial of a single person who has been personally affected by a commonly fatal disease or has overcome a serious illness?

(Editor's note: We don't suggest you crash your airplane or come down with cancer just to be more interesting).

Statistics

In the absence of individual testimony, statistics can be otherwise powerful. Using statistical evidence or numerical facts arranged for analysis and interpretation are great for technical people and financial folks. They can also simplify complicated information for people that aren't technically oriented.

Statistics may also point out some real surprises or interesting findings that get the audience's attention. However, don't fall in the trap of presenting too many statistics or numbers at once. You could lose or confuse the audience. You may also jeopardize your own believability, if you yourself don't fully understand the statistics being presented.

And don't think that numbers alone are going to convince anyone. If you want people to listen to your numbers, you need to wrap them in something more interesting, such as the story behind the numbers. You have to humanize them. A million of anything is not easy for humans to picture or comprehend. A billion is almost impossible. But if you stood a billion barrels of oil side by side, they would circle the earth almost 16 times. That's a lot of oil!

Keep in mind that Mark Twain did say this: *"There are three kinds of lies: lies, damned lies and statistics."* Be sure when using statistics that you've researched them to the point that they're not only true, but also that they don't manipulate the truth to fit your argument.

Here's a true-story example from a participant:

"When proofreading an article for a health care company, I read that 1 in 3 women will die of heart failure. I nearly fell out of my chair because I happen to have two sisters and I immediately wondered which of the three of us is likely to be it.

Luckily, I had a doctor appointment that week and I raised the question. My doctor said that it is a true statement, but consider the facts: If by the time you get to be very old, and cancer didn't get you or you didn't get hit by a bus, you have to die somehow. When you die, the last thing to happen is that your heart stops (i.e., heart failure). So the question isn't which will be the "lucky" one to live that long, but who are the unlucky two that will die of something else? (Yes, there are some premature deaths involving heart failure, but most are related to natural causes.)"

The moral of the story is, don't just arbitrarily cut and paste statistics. Be sure you understand the context in which they are given and use them appropriately. Remember to keep things simple, be clear, and be concise so we can all relish in the wisdom of your easy-to-understand message.

Examples

Throughout this book, we share stories from our presentation experiences to show what works and what doesn't. By having examples, it's easier to grasp and think, "Yes, this could work here too." People are more open to attempt something if they know it has worked before, especially if the situation is similar.

If you use an example from a similar industry or a different department in your company, and the example seems "close to home", it makes it so much easier to sell your idea. Try hard to make your example as tightly paralleled to your solution/recommendation as possible.

Analogy

Alluding to how your new idea is similar to an idea that

everybody knows can paint the big picture of understanding. The classic "tip-of-the-iceberg" analogy, though a cliché, is commonly used in business to warn against an impending larger doom that lurks just below the surface.

The right analogy can make a lasting impression with listeners and the image of that iceberg, or "not seeing the forest for the trees", will hopefully be something that is burned into your audience's memory.

Most people learn by relating new information to something similar that they already know. Metaphors (words) and analogies (actions) are the building blocks of all learning.

For some great examples of helping people learn new things by relating them to things they know, check out www.AnneMiller.com and sign up for her free Metaphor Minute newsletter.

Benefits to the Audience

Make sure your audience is aware of how your point has direct meaning to them. For example, "What this means to you is…"greater earnings in the future", or "more opportunities for growth within the organization", or, on everyone's mind, "job security". Whatever that positive connection to the audience is, make it very clear.

> **Essential Point:** Too many less-than-seasoned sales-people do a great job of pointing out their product's *features* and *advantages*, but neglect

> the only part of real interest to the customer, which is the *benefit* they will derive from using a product with all these great features and advantages.

Sales organizations often teach the FAB concept: The Feature is what the product *is*. The Advantage is what the product *does*. The Benefit is what the product *does for you*, the consumer. Classic example: windshield wipers.

Feature: A device that swings a rubber blade back and forth across your windshield at varying speeds.

Advantage: Clears the windshield of water, ice, or other road spray.

Benefit: Allows the driver to operate the vehicle in any meteorological condition. In other words, you can see where you're going in the rain.

Typically, too much presentation time is devoted to promoting features and advantages. Less frequently do we see space devoted to what exactly all the cool stuff can do to make the client's life easier, or more secure, or more profitable. Don't waste your audience's time telling them what you can do. Tell them what you can do for *them*.

Keep your presentation tuned to their favorite radio station, WIIFM - "What's In It For Me?" It's the only one your audience is ever listening to.

Call to Action / Next Steps

You've gotten them motivated. You've excited them. You've done it all with great style and panache. Now, what do you want them to do? Don't forget to finish your job by asking them to do some things for you. Be as specific as possible.

Don't end your presentation like this:

> *"Thanks for your support"… "I appreciate your time, let's stay in touch"… "Please do what you can".*

Instead, use phrasing such as:

> *"I need everyone to write his or her congressperson today."*

And have that address in a handout or up on the screen.

Or:
> *"At the end of the month we'll be meeting again, so please e-mail your suggestions. I need at least two paragraphs from everyone, on my desk by the 15th."*

Perhaps you need to mention what criteria must be met, specifically who will be responsible for what, and how this all will be measured. Either way, ensure your message is on top of the in-basket and not at the bottom of the round file. Be precise; ask for specifics.

End with a Bang

Your last words should leave your audience inspired or with something to think about. If you've done everything right, your audience will have stayed with you

every step of the way. But even if you've lost a few of them in the middle, your audience will especially remember the beginning and the end.

Think of an Olympic gymnast, who spins her lithe little body around the parallel bars and into seemingly impossible airborne positions: what does she always have to do to get the points? She has to *stick* the landing.

Stick the landing with your next presentation by summing up with a reference that alludes to, or makes whole, your unforgettable grabber.

"Ladies and gentlemen, I opened this talk today with the outrageous claim that we could raise productivity in your department by over 25% in just 12 months." [Your Grabber]

"I ask you now: does anyone here not believe with what you've learned, 50% is not within reach?" [Bang]

Give your audience something to talk about after they leave your talk.

Points to Remember

- You have 30 seconds to let them know that this presentation is not going to be like ones the you've suffered through before.

- Don't make your next presentation just a stream-of-consciousness data dump. Instead, organize it around a formula that grabs their attention in the beginning, directs their attention to a pre-designated solution through the middle, and wraps it up into a neat bundle at the end. Less than ½ hour, skip the Agenda.

- Let them know exactly where you're going from the beginning so they can put everything you say into a preformed context.

- Give them evidence that they can relate to and hopefully has direct benefit to them.

- Close with a call to action that, no matter how small, gives them a reason to keep thinking about your presentation after they leave the room.

"We are the hurdles we leap to be ourselves".
- Michael McClure

Suggested Exercises

This exercise requires you to think rather than act. It also provides a good framework to keep in mind when constructing future presentations. The goals of this exercise are to help you:

- Organize your thoughts.
- Use a format that will get the audiences' attention.
- End the presentation on a high note.

Think about a presentation that you will be giving or that you have given before. Reflect on it and write down these anchoring concepts:

1. The "Grabber" (A thought provoking question or statement)
2. Problem/Opportunity (Make sure it's something everyone can relate to)
3. Solution/Recommendation ("Here's something I'd like you to think about…")
4. Choose One Type of Evidence (Personal, Statistics, Example, Analogy)
5. Benefits to The Audience (What this means to you is…)
6. Call to Action/Next Steps (Nail down the specifics)
7. Ending with a "Bang" (Revisit the "grabber" or encapsulate key points)

Chapter 7:
Introduction to Design

Columbia

Very early on a late January morning in 2003, seven astronauts aboard the Space Shuttle Columbia were circling the earth, donning their gear, and looking forward to coming home after 12 days in space. They were not aware, nor would they ever be aware, that back on earth a debate had been raging at various levels inside and outside of NASA over the advisability of clearing Columbia for the hazards of re-entry.

Boeing engineers in the ad hoc Debris Assessment Team had been fruitlessly seeking the ear of persons of authority in the Mission Management Team, in a desperate attempt to get them to understand that a catastrophe might quickly unfold.

These highly educated people, these engineers — or rather, these rocket scientists — had tried to convince their superiors — er... executive rocket scientists — that a 1.67-pound block of high-tech

Styrofoam had likely inflicted enough damage to either the protective tiles or the wing to put into question the ship's survivability upon contact with the super-heated gases that would soon be created by friction with the atmosphere.

Sadly, the seven souls aloft had put their faith in rocket science, when what they really needed was a brain surgeon. The neurosurgeon would have at least understood that the human brain, being neatly sliced in two as it is, is often much more susceptible to persuasion when presented with right-brain type information rather than the strictly (and even over-the-top) left-brain evidence that the rocket scientists had used to no avail.

Over the course of five days, the Debris Assessment Team had delivered three presentations, consisting of a total of 28 slides that attempted to show that they had studied both the evidence available about Columbia and the evidence on all the foam that had ever fallen off any of the previous shuttles.

For almost a decade, NASA scientists had been aware of the spray-on foam insulation's (referred to in the slides as SOFI) tendency to flake off from the main fuel tank under the rigors of takeoff. The errant foam was almost always from the areas where complicated surfaces required manual application, rather than by the precise computer-controlled process that applied the foam to the other 99 percent of the tank.

One of these areas, known as the "bipod ramp" and referred to in the presentations as simply the "ramp", was unfortunately well-suited to commit major damage with flying foam owing to its location near the forward tip of the shuttle. Foam detaching from this point, given the relative speed of the shuttle in its path, could strike with a force exceeding that of a brick shot from a cannon at short range.

Unfortunately, shuttle program manager Ronald Dittemore didn't completely understand the physics involved. Dittemore was the face and voice of NASA in the first week after the accident. That is until he revealed a lack of respect for scientific inquiry during a press conference by holding up a sample of SOFI and saying to the world, "I'm sorry, but nobody's ever going to convince me that a piece of foam could bring down a space shuttle!"

Although the problem of foam debris breaking off and striking the hull at takeoff had been significant enough to have NASA commission a quantifying test, referred to in the slides as Crater, the rocket scientists suspected that the current parameters of the problem were not like anything they had studied before.

The mindset in place with the NASA Mission Management Team at the time was that yes, we know foam falls off and damages tiles, but that is an issue of maintenance, not safety-of-flight. Its an issue for the turn-around crew. Let's not worry our pretty little heads about the extra work the clean-up guys will have when the ship returns to the hanger.

So when the rocket scientists pitched their arguments to the executive rocket scientists, even though all the information that was needed to make their arguments was included in the slides, the slides themselves were put together in such a way that even executive rocket scientists couldn't see it. The decision makers didn't buy the pitch, the order to continue re-entry as planned was given, and a couple of days later, seven people died.

This is a truly tragic story, made all the more so by the fact it was the second time (the first being the *Challenger* disaster of 1986) NASA decision makers failed to heed the warnings of their own experts. And yet as you will see in the next chapters, the reason the engineers failed to convince the decision-makers is not because of the *content* of the information presented, but rather the *form* in which the content was presented. A presentation design problem.

It is apparent from the volume of information in the slides that the Boeing rocket scientists had done an admirable job of researching the problem. And having conducted such exhaustive research, it is reasonable to assume that they thought they were doing their job by presenting ALL of it to the people who would ultimately decide if their take on the evidence was sound. They no doubt believed that the key was in the content.

In chapter 9, we'll take a look at an actual slide from the presentation that doomed these seven souls, and if you indeed read and take to heart the rules we uncover here, you will see why the experts failed to make their case. For now, understand that, to make a convincing argument, the form of your content is just as critical as the content itself.

Mimicking Your Boss's Mistakes

We often find that presenters inherit the mistakes that their bosses make. When asked to give a presentation, they are often given the same materials that the last presenter (often the boss) used. After all, if it's good enough for the boss, it's good enough for them, right? So the "template" these presenters use is based on one created by somebody who very likely never took a course in presentation design, but likely was also mimicking yet another boss. And with each progression up the corporate ladder, the situation repeats — and the problems compound.

At PublicSpeakingSkills.com, we have worked with people from all different industries for over fifteen years, helping them improve, among other things, their presentation delivery skills. We've had many presenters come to us from corporate cultures that have developed evermore complicated — read "incomprehensible" — corporate presentations that not only make their jobs more difficult, but also cruelly bear the approval of upper management.

We are often told that a group needs serious help with their delivery skills, only to discover that they're working with slides that not even a great presenter could successfully deliver.

Breaking this vicious circle is not easy, as most corporate clients, until shown otherwise, simply don't think their slides stink. But of the literally thousands of slides that we see every year, fewer than 5% pass the Knowledge Transfer smell test. Worse, most corporate presentations today actually work *against* creating anything like Knowledge Transfer, and instead do their best to get in the way of it.

We take presentation design seriously, because we know how important a role it plays in proper presentation delivery. Like a lot of things in life or business, a little training never hurts.

First to Know

Proper presentation design begins with a fundamental understanding of what happens each time the presenter presses a button and brings up a new visual. But first, we have to understand a very basic tenet of human nature — that is, we have a pervasive and inherent need to be "the first to know".

Curiosity is a survival instinct. We have evolved as creatures who need to learn what we can quickly. This same desire that humans have — to be *the first to know* — translates to every event that involves new information uptake. During a presentation, audience members want the same control, and are generally unwilling to wait for you, the presenter, to *help* them be the first to know.

Figure 7.1 When the presenter has *cleared* the slide, thus eliminating any curiosity about it, the audience will turn their attention back to him...

Only after their curiosity about a slide has been satisfied will audience members turn their attention away from the screen and back to the presenter.

But, when a new slide appears, all eyes, like moths to the flame, tune to the new image, and immediately begin the race to be *the first to know* what the next slide is all about. It's not their fault - they're human!

Figure 7.2 ...But when new information appears, until the audience has determined what all the elements mean, the presenter is essentially not there.

At this point you might as well not be there. Oh sure, you can act as most do and begin to describe the elements in the slide, but for all intents and purposes, it matters little what you do. You could drop your pants. You could leave the room. You could tell off-color jokes. But until the audience has determined *for themselves* exactly what all the data and word tracks on the screen mean, you have exactly 0% of their attention.

> **Essential Point:** Only when every member of the audience is thoroughly convinced that he knows what *all* the elements on the slide mean will they lend their attention back to what you are saying. Until then, you're "vaporized"!

When you fill a slide with too much content, it takes the audience that much longer to get around to paying attention to you. The reading process itself is even delayed, because the viewer first tries to decide where to begin, and which piece of information is most important. Clues to the relative value of the information are often erroneous, however, as audiences base them on properties such as the size of the type or placement on the screen.

Gone in 60 Seconds

Consider how long it will take the average person to grasp all the information you have on your slide. The longer it takes the average person to absorb and assimilate the information, the greater the chance you have to lose your audience.

People process information at different rates; faster processors will take a shorter time and the slower processors will take longer. Before you know it, you've got an audience working at three or four or five different speeds, and therefore at different portions of the screen.

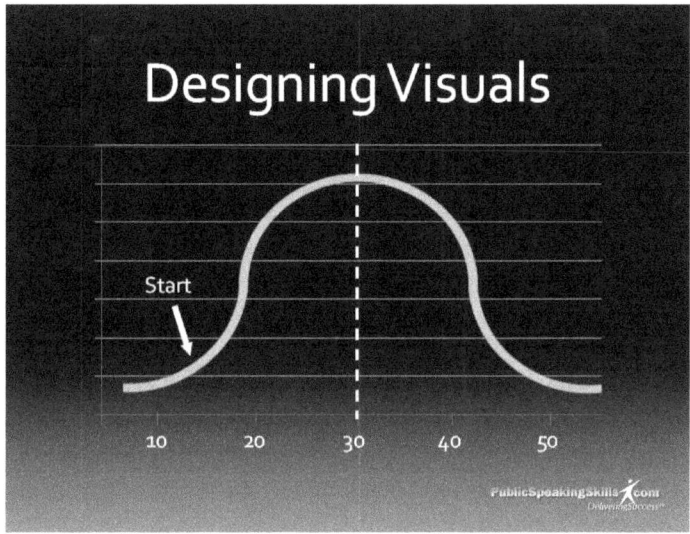

Figure 7.3 Most human group behavior can be described by a bell curve, including the amount of time it takes audience members to read and digest a slide.

If the time it takes the *average* reader to absorb the info on the screen is 30 seconds, then a classic bell curve will tell you that 20% of the audience is going to read it all in 20 seconds, and 20% will take 40 seconds. Another aggregate 20 will fall into either the 10- or the 60-second range. And when we calculate it all, we know that we have the audience broken down into at least 5 groups of speed lanes. Add you, the presenter, who begins talking at a new, arbitrary point. To whom are you speaking?

Chance tells us you're speaking to the largest group; let's say the 40% who read at an average pace. That leaves 60% (a landslide in political terms) either way ahead or way behind you.

But Wait! There's More!

Actually, it gets worse! As much as you might be totally in love with the design of a slide you may have spent hours composing, audiences rarely find your stuff as captivating. Because the presentation is important to you, it's easy to believe that everyone will be engrossed in the action on the screen, thus giving the event their entire attention.

Be honest. Have you ever sat through a colleague's presentation and found yourself thinking about something other than the material he was sweating blood to deliver? A report that's due later that day? Your weekend plans? Lunch?

No audience member, no matter how captivating you might believe you are, ever gives a presenter 100% of her attention. Human minds don't work that way. Long before Windows, we were multi-taskers.

So what does this tell us? There is only one truly viable solution. Limit, by all means possible, the amount of information released with each click of your mouse. Develop the discipline to hold back.

First, the less time it takes the audience to discern the new information; the sooner they'll get back to listening to you, and engaging with you.

Second, the less time it takes the aggregate audience to comprehend the content, the less discrepancy between the fast learners and the slow.

Third, and most important, if your content consists only of graphics and talking points in headline-style phrases, the audience will soon realize that they must listen to you to get the rest of the information. They will conclude the only way they can hope to be *the first to know* is to turn their attention to you, and have it spoon fed to them. And this is exactly where you want them to be!

If you put everything you want them to know up on the screen, and spell it out longhand, you are training the audience to look to the screen for their information. Humans recognize patterns quickly, and as soon as the screen becomes the pattern, that's where they'll go. But most of them will be reading one thing while you're speaking to another.

The 10-Second Rule

The rule of thumb? Make sure with each passing image, it never takes longer than 10 seconds for the audience to "clear the slide". By clearing the slide we mean removing the curiosity. Have no more than 10 seconds of material — bullet point, graphic, chart, etc. — appear at one time.

This 10-second rule is not just a good idea. It is the foundation upon which all the other rules are based. All too often we see slides that don't come near this rule. At PublicSpeakingSkills.com, we review thousands of PowerPoint® slides every year. From our experience, barely one in a hundred comes close to the requisite time; most take 60 seconds or more for the audience to decipher the material! And in 60 seconds, they're gone!

If you can deliver each new element that appears on the screen in 10 seconds or less, you'll never have to worry about losing someone to the reading difference bell-curve. At worse, a 50% difference will mean an additional 5 seconds, and that can be managed with simply an additional pause or two. Remember that the goal is to get them in the habit of looking to you as the dispenser of the information.

> **Essential Point:** By limiting the time you spend delivering from the screen, you expand your opportunity to bond with the audience. It is only from within this bond that true knowledge transfer takes place. That is the signal hallmark of all good presentations.

The Presentation – A Unique Art Form

Although Salvador Dali is reported to have died in 1989, and William Shakespeare quite a few years prior, they both continue to produce most of the presentations foisted on corporate America's audiences today.

Presenters evidently collaborate with Mr. Shakespeare, penning the endless pages of tiny type for which he is noted, while Señor Dali supplies the surrealistic images that can't possibly be understood without the presenter leading an entire day-long discussion on abstract art appreciation.

When Shakespeare put together his first blockbusters, he didn't have Jerry Bruckheimer to wow the crowds with great pyrotechnics; he had to rely on extended and cleverly convoluted use of the spoken word. Any of Dali's paintings, or those of other Surrealists, (the school he founded) can provide long periods of entertainment as the observer seeks the hidden meanings in the myriad of abstract images.

But these guys have got to get out of the presentation business! As tempting as it is for most of us to cut and paste our way from our other MS Office files to a finished presentation, the presentation is its own unique media. And while the rules of good design transcend many forms of message, there are reasons why the stuff we put on the screen must conform to rules that don't necessarily apply to other forms of communication.

The most common characteristic among the presentations that our corporate customers send us for review and revision is that they attempt to structure their arguments on the screen in the same way they do in their handouts. That is, they design their presentations to work as a piece to be read and studied at one's leisure.

Unfortunately, what may work well for one, does not work well for many. People read at their own speeds. With a written document, readers can skip ahead or go back and re-read. They can choose which topics to concentrate on and which to ignore. They are not limited to a linear approach.

Consider reading a magazine. You can read them front to back or vice versa. You can read every article straight through, or start another when the first one is continued on page 197. Most people have a pretty private relationship with their favorite magazine. Now imagine if the only way you could read a magazine was in concert with a dozen or so other readers. Who would determine the page order? How long would the group spend on one page before moving on to another? Does this sound like fun to you?

Although from time to time Hollywood is able to create a moneymaker from an original script, the overwhelming majority of movies that have ever been made started life as best-selling books. The key to making a great movie from a great book is finding the core elements of the book that tell the story, and of course allowing the visual elements to do as much of the story-telling as possible.

Have you ever read a novel and then watched the movie? Did you notice the kind of slaughter a scriptwriter must commit to get the dialogue and action down to two hours? The Hollywood flop list is full of attempts to include more material from the book than necessary because it means the film ran way too long. People don't want to sit through three hours of onscreen "entertainment", regardless of how much more filling the story may be. Literal rendering of books to film doesn't work because of the volume of content.

For many of the same reasons, presentations written to also work as handouts become disasters on the screen. No one can sit through the same quantity of information from a screen than they can from a written document. Your job as presenter is to take the material you want your audience to really comprehend and put it forth in a way so everyone in the group, regardless of their perception rate, is digesting it at the same time.

The Root of all PowerPoint® Evil

A little history: In 1984, former Berkeley PhD. student Bob Gaskins left his job as head of computer research at Bell-Northern Research and joined another Mountain View, California software firm, Forethought Inc. in return for limited monetary compensation and a good deal of company stock. In hindsight, Forethought was a good move. That same year, in cooperation with software developer Dennis Austin, they began work on a program they originally called Presenter. Years later, Gaskins would find an old business plan from that time describing the concept behind the new software. One phrase in the short document read, *"Allows the content-originator to control the presentation."*

PowerPoint® 1.0 was launched in April 1987, a Macintosh-only product that allowed non-designers to put together simple black-and-white overheads without the need for a corporate graphics department. Later that same year Gaskins and his colleagues sold Forethought to Microsoft for cash and stock.

Modern business would never be the same again. Immediately, business presenters who had little or no background in design *fundamentals* were now able to do what thousands of recently empowered "desktop" publishers could do: produce very technically competent garbage. And the more audiences saw this garbage, the more they wanted to create garbage of their own.

Today, the root of the problem with most presentations is that for most corporate applications, the software is no longer used to allow the content-originator to control the presentation, but rather to be the main communication tool throughout the organization, both laterally and vertically. Weekly reports, quarterly reports, quality control reports and new programs from the human resources department are expected to be written in PowerPoint®, and disseminated often without a presenter attached.

And it is this total misuse of the original product that has led to the acceptance of PowerPoint® files as *documents* rather than *visual aids*. Documents are necessary to deliver the volume and detail required to distribute many types of information. Visual aids are necessary to keep the attention of the 75% of all audience members who are primarily *visual* learners. But documents should never be asked to work as visual aids, and vice-versa.

To return to our magazine analogy, think of the amount of information an advertising agency would include in a full-page ad in a car enthusiast magazine for a new BMW convertible. The page would contain a picture of the vehicle, to be sure, but would also contain quite a bit of copy detailing the car's horsepower, torque, turning radius, suspension enhancements, new luxury features – in short, the volume of information that a car enthusiast would enjoy reading. In most cases, the more the better.

But would the ad agency that created the magazine copy use that very same ad on a billboard? Of course not. A billboard is meant to deliver information in the exceedingly short period of time that it is in front of the audience's eyes as they speed past. The billboard would also have a captivating photo of the new car, but instead of the detailed magazine copy it would have two words in large, bold print:

GETS CHICKS

And that's it. Magazines are a proper venue for documents. Billboards, which are designed to stir interest enough so that you will seek out more information the next time you come across a document on that product, are visual aids. Neither could ever serve the other's purpose, and ad agencies, learned in transferring information visually, would never try.

Solution: Two Files

The solution, therefore, is to have one file of slides that you project and speak to during your live presentation, and another file of slides to hand-out. Before you cry that that's more work, here's what we do: Start every new presentation by writing out all your thoughts in complete sentence format. Put in every thing you can think of, because a document meant to be read can rarely have too much information – the reader, remember, has a choice of how much time and effort she will devote to your details.

The act of writing everything out in sentences will help you in your delivery, because these are the words that will come to mind when you bring up your (edited) bullet-points. Save this document as your hand-out or pass-around.

For the on-screen file, start with this wordy and information-rich document and take out your machete.

You will first whittle down the number of ideas that you'll have time to develop fully in your allotted time. Once you've edited the content to those points you know for sure the audience will actually remember when your presentation is over, you then attack each slide to remove extraneous words in the lines you have kept.

By attack, we mean leave standing the absolute fewest number of words (or elements in a graph or graphics, etc.) that it takes to cue the audience as to where you're going, and to cue you to speak from your own internal knowledge base. If you're using pictures, keep in mind that one large one is generally more effective than many smaller ones.

By keeping screen content to a minimum, you maximize not only your audience's need to get the information directly from you - you also maximize the freedom you have to say whatever comes to mind at the moment.

The rules set forth in the next chapter ensure that with each slide you present, you are not introducing any opportunities for audience members to fall off the pace.

"Discovery consists of seeing what everybody has seen and thinking what nobody has thought."

\- Albert Szent-Gyorgyi

Points to Remember

- To make a convincing argument, the form of your content is just as critical as the content itself.
- Never be too shy to try to improve what your boss gives you.
- Humans have a pervasive and inherent need to be "the first to know". Thus your audience won't wait for you to explain – they'll try to figure it all for themselves first.
- Limit the content that comes up with any one click of the mouse to take no more than 10 seconds for the audience to grasp.
- Don't try to make one file serve as both an information document and a set of visual aids. It simply doesn't work.
- The less you put on the screen, the more value you, the presenter, add to the presentation.

Suggested Exercises

1. Open your last presentation. With every bullet point, remove 3 things:

a. All instances of the verb to be – is, are, will be, etc.

b. All articles – a, an, the, etc.

c. Any word or phrase you wouldn't read in a headline.

Then if you have duplicate words, restructure your bullet points so you only have to use the duplicated word once.

2. If any slide contains more information than the average person would take more than 10 seconds to comprehend before returning their attention to you:

a. Depending on your version, select Duplicate Slide.

b. Split the contents of the slide into two and apply the 10-second rule to each.

c. Continue to split each slide until you're certain you're not exceeding 10 seconds.

*"Thunder is good,
thunder is impressive;
but it is lighting that does all the work".*

\- Mark Twain

Chapter 8:
The 7 Rules of Visual Design

The rules set forth in this chapter ensure that with every slide you present, you are not introducing opportunities to let any member of your audience fall off the pace. Follow these rules, and you will pretty much guarantee that presenter and audience will be on the same page, the same wavelength, every step of the way.

So let's look at some basic rules:

1. Favor Right-Brain information
2. K.I.S.S. - Less is More
3. One concept per visual
4. Use proper builds
5. Be colorful - Light on dark
6. Avoid boring fonts
7. Maintain paragraph integrity

We'll examine these rules one-by-one, in the classic David Letterman style.

Rule 7: Maintain paragraph integrity

Size Matters

One of the most common mistakes in presentation design is the seemingly cavalier approach designers take to font size discipline. And here, Microsoft is very much to blame, for unless you uncheck the default value under *Options*, PowerPoint® will automatically resize your font to fit the text box. Thus we end up with a slide like this:

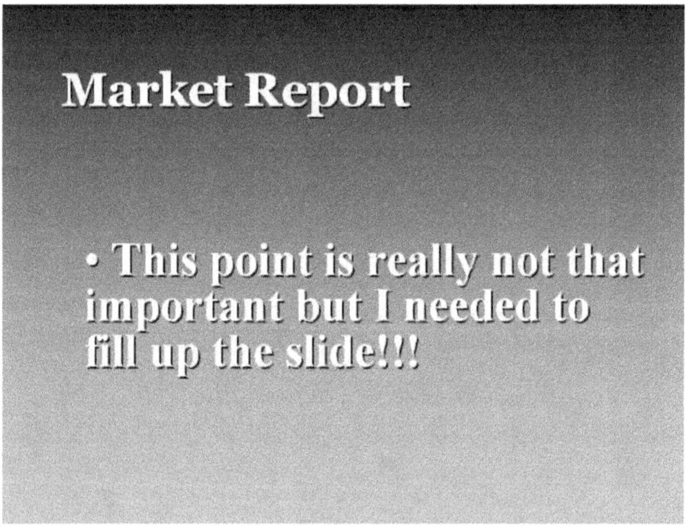

Figure 8.1 Ever notice slides sometimes contain beefed-up font sizes to fill the real estate...

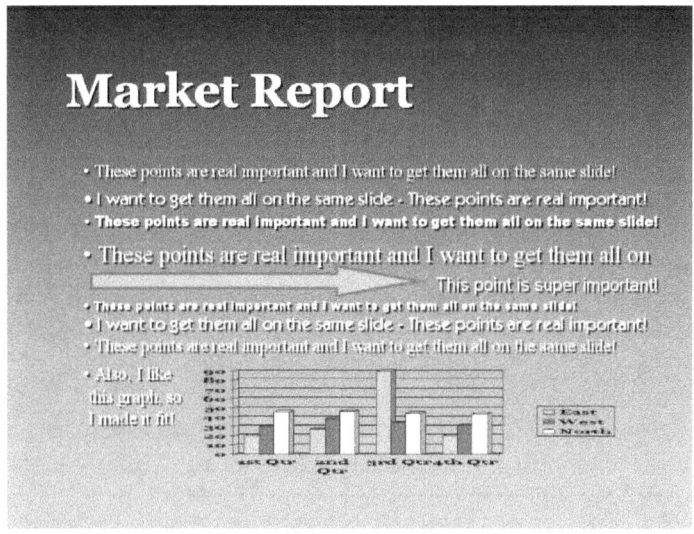

Figure 8.2 ... and are inevitably followed by a slide with font sizes squeezed down to fit on the page.

The problem with violating what's known as "paragraph integrity" is that humans innately relate font size to message importance. Your audience will translate large text as a headline and small text as copy. Words in large type are treated as more important than words in smaller type. This is not an unreasonable assumption considering all other media do it that way.

You absolutely want to reduce the amount of energy and bandwidth your audience's brains need for housekeeping functions such as interpreting what the *properties* of the data might mean. Fonts contain a great deal of information that the brain interprets on a subconscious level. Font properties include the style, size, color, and case. In addition, the brain looks for clues such as the location of the data (stuff at the top of the screen is probably more important), its proximity to other data (if it's close, it's probably related), and the volume of the data relative to the total volume of information projected on the screen.

When your audience sees consistencies in font properties from one slide to the next, the amount of brainwork they devote to filtering and interpreting is reduced, and they can devote more resources to digesting your message – to buying in to your point of view.

Remember, these things happen subconsciously, at a level you can't work against (but you can certainly work with). So follow these guidelines:

All 1st Level paragraphs must be the same size in every slide
All 2nd Level paragraphs must be smaller & a different color
Don't go beyond the 3rd Level, nor smaller than 20 points

When all information of the same importance is of the same size, your audience won't need to think harder. You can take this concept one step further by ensuring that all material of the same nature is the same color. For example, if you use a lot of numbers in your bullet points, make them all one color, different from the text. Once your audience recognizes this pattern, they'll spend less time digging through the text to find their figures.

By using font properties to assign importance and relational attributes to your text, the text properties will become visuals. You will thus engage the right brain of your audience, and uptake will be quicker, clearer, and longer lasting. More on right-brain / left brain in the next chapter.

Don't Jerk Me Around

Avoid putting your audience through "the jerk" as you move from slide to slide. Each time a new slide appears, your audience has to process all that is new. But we often see successions of slides where the headline or a graph might be the same, but they move fractions of an inch with each new slide. When that happens, the audience wastes a lot of brain power deciphering the "new" information, while not adding to their knowledge.

On the other hand, any content that remains the same in the next slide (i.e., the same data – text or graphics – in the same location) can be omitted from the deciphering process because it has already been deciphered.

Only content that is new to the slide should change or move between slides. Everything else should be in the exact same position it was on the slide before it. If the headline or logo moves even just slightly, the eye sees that jerk of change and the brain must reprocess it.

To create content that stays in place in Microsoft PowerPoint®, avoid ever using the New Slide feature. Instead, use Duplicate Slide when creating a new slide. Then you can change the content without changing the content's properties. Swiping the old text and replacing with new text assures that the new content will always at least begin in the same location as the previous content. Also, unlike other Microsoft Office products, when you copy an object from one slide and paste it into another, it places it in exactly the same spot as the slide from which it was copied.

Rule 6: Avoid Boring Fonts

Rarely is there a need to use more than two different fonts in any presentation. But you do not have to stick with the same old dull Times New Roman and Arial.

Everybody uses these two fonts. You can make your presentation really stand out by choosing another font.

Two optional fonts that every Windows system has resident are Tahoma and Verdana. Verdana is actually the font of the Internet – something like three-quarters of all websites use it. You can easily see how a different font can change the "feel" of your presentation in PowerPoint® by choosing the Format menu and then selecting Change Fonts. The change will be global.

The one word of caution here is that you never want to use a font that requires any effort to read, such as the many fancy fonts like scripts or antiques. Like most everything else in slide design, simpler is generally better. Then, to be sure the font you've chosen will be the font displayed on any platform (such as somebody else's computer), select Embed True Type Fonts. Your font will then become part of the presentation, although it won't add significantly to your file size.

Rule 5: Be Colorful

Watch a lot of black-and-white television these days? Although black-and-white works as an art form, humans tend to like color. Even the old-guard newspapers like the New York Times and the Wall Street Journal finally concluded that to avoid losing readers to more modern media, they had to colorize. While humans can discern no more than 24 shades of gray, they can see millions of colors. We've evolved our sense of color to survive.

If you plan to print your presentation as a handout, and find that the color does not print well, consider making a separate copy of your presentation for print purposes using different shades and colors. Or, simply choose "Print B&W" from the initial Print dialogue box. Print copies are read differently from screen copies. The screen copy, remember, is a *visual* aid.

Color can actually help the presenter get her point across more easily. Using different colors can make points on the slide stand out much better than other contrivances like bold or underlining, because color is processed by our non-filtering right brains.

Use at least two colors to generate interest; use three to excite. But using more than four colors can actually distract attention. Microsoft provides "palettes" with their templates, but be careful not to overwhelm.

Use color to maintain a consistency with your visuals. By limiting your palette, by keeping all the information of a similar kind in similar color, your audience will recognize the consistency by about the third slide. This will ease the amount of effort their brains have to exert to understand your message, thus increasing retention.

Rule 4: Use Proper Builds

Builds, also known as animations, allow you to totally

control the flow of information to your audience, so we say: use them! But you must use them wisely.

With all that we preach about limiting the amount of information that you throw at your audience at any one time, you would think that being able to "build" your onscreen argument one idea at a time would be a good thing. And it is, right up until it becomes too much of a good thing. Without a good sense of design, animations can quickly overwhelm and destroy an otherwise well planned presentation.

The trick is to introduce new concepts one at a time in a way that does not draw more attention to the build than to the concept itself.

Builds are essential elements in turning overly busy slides into ones that audiences can easily follow. Like other elements of good design, a proper build should never announce itself. Rather, the presentation should have subtle transitions from one concept to the next.

The bottom line here is that most slides do one of two things: either all the information appears at once without giving the audience a chance to digest it at a reasonable pace, or the information itself is drowned out by the actions the designer uses to bring it onto the screen. You need to find the gentle middle ground that works for both the audience and presenter alike.

Rule 3: One Concept per Visual

Your visual is not as simple as it can be if it contains more than one concept.

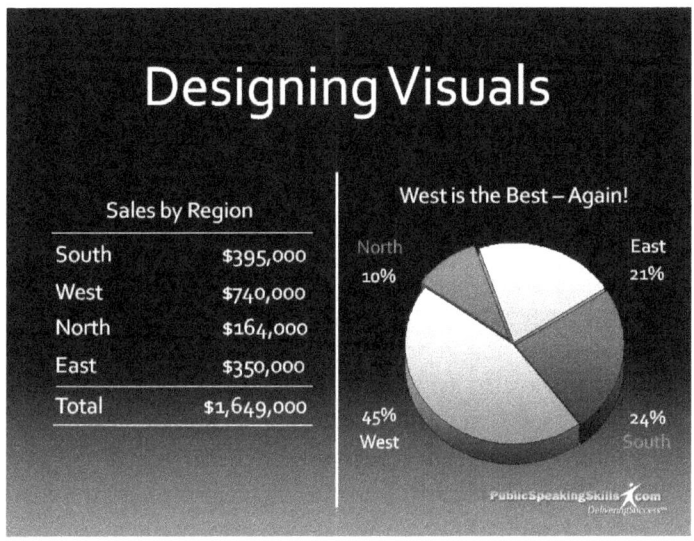

Figure 8.3 When comparing two concepts, introduce each as a separate visual, and then create a third visual to compare them. (Or, you can "build" each visual on the same slide.)

Figure 8.3 compares the difference in speed of graphs to charts in conveying the same data. But did you know that upon first glance? Was the concept self-evident? If not, you may have spent time and precious attention trying to interpret the visual.

This particular visual is actually the third slide in the series. The first one contains only the chart. When shown, the presenter explains if you need to show data such as sales figures, it helps if you provide good organization, such as a chart. Then he brings up the second slide, and discusses how a graph can get the same message across much more quickly, especially if we title the graph with an action phrase instead of a generic description (what the data *shows* rather than what it *is*).

Only after he's made those separate points (each *one* concept), does he bring them together to introduce the *third* concept, which is the comparison. In this fashion, the audience can be completely in tune.

Remember that as audience members race to be the "first to know", they not only attempt to read everything as quickly as possible, they also create a hierarchy of importance of the data. When there is more than one concept appearing at the same time, they not only try to figure out the concepts, they try to determine which one deserves most of their attention. This extra time and effort on the part of the audience acts as a drag on presentation flow, and explains why a properly designed 45-slide presentation, broken down into one concept per slide, can take less time to present than the same information packed into 15.

Rule 2: Less is More

Einstein once said that *"an explanation should be as simple as possible, but no simpler"*. Be careful not to interpret "Keep-it-Simple" as "Keep it Simple-minded". As Edward Tufte says, don't assume that your audience has gotten dumber just to come hear you speak. Simple refers to nothing more than the *design* of individual slides.

You may be giving a presentation on the latest successful techniques in human cloning, and that's not likely to lend itself to an 8th-grade reading level. But even the most intricate subjects of scientific or engineering presentations have to be designed in a way most people will "get" right away.

Your job as presentation designer is to create an interactive "document" that 1) supports the ideas, concepts, or arguments you need to put forth, and 2) keys the audience to what you're going to talk about just before you fulfill your role in the process, which is to *deliver the presentation*.

> **Essential Point**: The presentation is not what's on the screen. It's also not what comes out of the presenter's mouth. The presentation is actually what takes place *in the mind of the listener.* You, as the presenter, are firing up their imaginations, memories and emotions. It takes a human to do that, not a screen. You need to both spoon feed and inspire the audience.

Never try to let the software and the hardware do all the work. You cannot be a casual moderator of the event. If you put everything you want the audience to know right into the body of the presentation, you omit the impact that you the speaker, the spoon-feeder, the inspirer, should be delivering to them.

Letting the audience read the presentation themselves insults them with bad, lazy design. You might as well give them a handout and send them on their way. (Not a very convincing way to state your argument.) Instead, just give a taste of the content on the slide and deliver the explanation verbally.

Self-Evident v. Self-Explanatory

What you bring up on the screen needs to *prepare* the audience for what you are just about to explain, and not attempt to be the explanation itself. The visual should, in the literal sense, speak for itself. It should not raise questions that start audience members off on a voyage of self-discovery.

If you can't make your visual self-evident, try for the next best, *self-explanatory*. A self-explanatory visual at least contains the explanation within the slide so that any would-be questions are immediately self-answered. For example, a graph with a legend that is large, clear and tied directly to the design of the graph, rather than a hard-to-read adjacent table, is self-explanatory. A self-evident graph would not need a legend at all. (Most Microsoft legends are only in their own minds).

To review, your presentation should be as simple as possible, but with respect for the intelligence of your audience, and no simpler. Because a well-designed presentation takes place in the minds of the audience, it's not what's up on the screen that determines how good your presentation is; it's how passionately you transfer that information to your listeners. And you can't do that really well unless you keep the focus on you rather than the screen. To keep the focus on you, you have to limit the amount of information on the screen, and Keep It Simple, Sweetheart.

Keeping it Simple

A full-page ad in a regional edition of the Wall Street Journal costs over $100,000. National editions costs even more. For that much money, would you devote the vast majority of that real estate to empty space?

Figure 8.4 Advertisers aren't wasting their money when they purchase full-page ads and then place only a few words on that page. Often, Less is More.

Absolutely. In many cases, when trying to make a strong impression, less is often more. In other words, the less ink spent on messages that might divert attention from the main point, the more impact the main message has.

When designing your slides (or for that matter your whole presentation), keep in mind that not only are audience's attention spans quite short, their retention is painfully low. When a major business seminar company from Shawnee Mission, Kansas did a six-month survey of thousands of attendees to their one-day programs, they learned that the typical adult learner retained only 10% of what he or she had learned a week later.

Your mission, then, is to determine not only if the piece of information you place on your slide is relevant, but also whether it will have staying power in the mind of your listener. Is it "need-to-know", or "nice-to-know"? Nice-to-know info makes for good talking matter to back up your main point, but only need-to-know material should ever appear on the screen.

The Power of White Space

Resist the urge to show and tell more. Seize the power of white space. The rule also applies to graphs and charts. Pie charts (actually graphs) with too many slices are hard to see and take too long to read. They won't remember more than five or six slices anyway, so why take away from the main point you need to make stick?

If you've got a VP of Self-Importance or something in the audience and you really might need to have ALL the data in your graph on hand, no problem. You simply create what is known as a "reference slide", which is derived from the simplified one you actually show, and insert a hyperlink to it from your main slide. You then "hide" that slide so if the VP doesn't call you out for more information, you simply cruise right on by it. Make your point more effective by limiting your displayed data to the stuff the audience will remember...

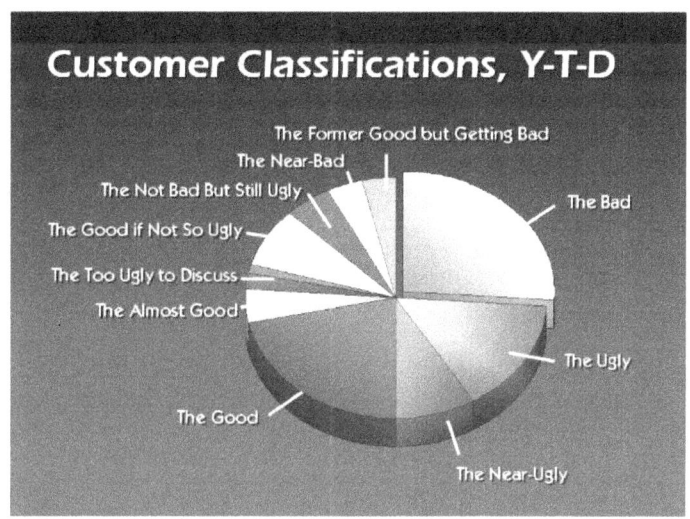

Figure 8.5 & 8.6: Rarely does your audience need to see all the data *on the screen* to understand your point. Details like those above are suitable for the handout you'll distribute *after* your talk. For the screen, stick to the main points.

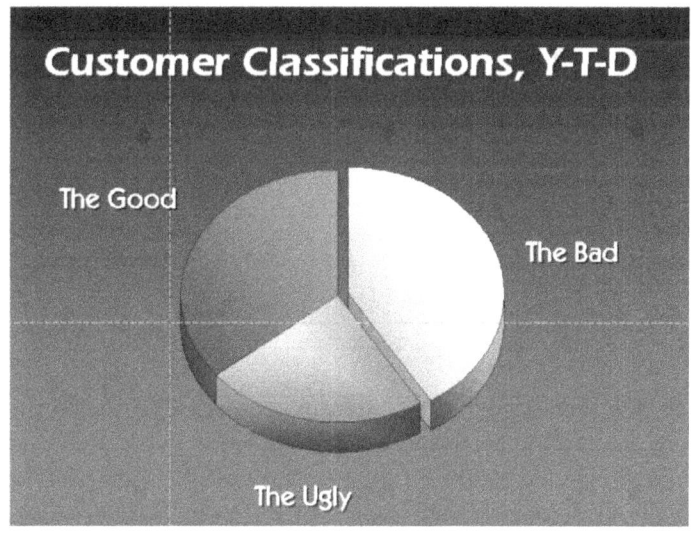

By restricting the quality of "screen-ink", as Dr. Tufte refers to it, you don't dilute the images burned into your listener's retina memory. Less information becomes more retention of the stuff you really want them to go home with. And if you say that the executive vice-president always insists on seeing ALL of the data, create what we call a 'reference slide" that does contain every slice and attach a hyperlink to it so you can reference it only if necessary.

The $20 Axiom

Talk is cheap, but words are not free. A meter doesn't click with every word you slap on the screen, but it would help if you thought of words as being precious, if not priceless. We suggest that you think of each word as costing you twenty dollars.

Why twenty bucks? Maybe because in the new millennium it doesn't mean as much to know "the value of *a* dollar" as it once did. Every word you include in your slide has a significant value — one that actually costs you something when you use it, and that rewards your frugality when you find a way to save one.

But edit you must! Cut! Chop! Reword! The typical first-draft slide has at least 50% more verbiage than necessary to get the point across.

Don't let the screen steal your thunder. If you've got something really great to say, don't share it with the screen. Share your wisdom with your audience after you've "cleared" the bullet point and you have the chance to step away from the screen and become naturally conversational.

Rule 1: Favor Right-Brain Information

When you pick up a magazine and leaf through it, what grabs your attention? It's not the text of the articles, is it? If you're a normal human, your eye is automatically attracted to the pictures or the graphics. To understand, let's review what you know about the old right brain, left-brain thing.

We humans have evolved with two different ways to deal with stimuli from the outside world so that we can react to it in the way most likely to keep us alive. It's a pretty neat trick if you think about it. Our right brain reacts to input such as colors, graphics, shapes and patterns instantly, without stopping to process the information first. In some cases, the hardwiring of our brains will cause input from the optic nerve to trigger physical actions without even discussing it with *you*!

Case in point: You and your friend are in the jungle, traversing a valley on a 200-foot Indiana Jones-type bridge over a deep river. Suddenly, a 20-foot snake slithers up from underneath the bridge. It's big enough to swallow you whole. From eons ago, your genes have held an image of this snake, and it's not a good image. It's yellow and orange with red spots down its back and a wide-open set of jaws still dripping blood stains from it's previous victim.

What do you do?

Many say, "Run!", but snakes get faster as they get bigger, and a human can't outrun a 20-foot snake. That's why you see those pictures of anaconda with whole wildebeests in their bellies. Now what?

Well, you don't stop and try to remember it's Latin genus name. You jump! Or, rather, your hamstrings retract and then your quadriceps extend, sending you into the river below. You don't enjoy falling or getting wet, but without asking, your brain decides it prefers living, and over you go. Your right brain just took charge.

Your right brain, reacting and responding to the type of information it understands, namely shapes and colors and patterns, sees the snake and determines that you're staring at Certain Death. It then checks out the surroundings, sees the water a hundred feet below, and concludes that a quick vertical exit would result in Probable Injury. It then takes a millisecond or so balancing the prospect of Certain Death vs. Probable Injury and says, "Go!"

You are wet, bruised and confused, but alive!

The Other Side

Now let's look at a similar scenario from your left brain's point of view. You survived the fall into the river, and have climbed back up the cliff. You're not a happy camper, and you still have to walk across that same darn swinging bridge.

This time, when you're halfway across, your friend yells

out, "Snake! Jump! Snake! Jump!" "Not again," you think, only this time, with the snake outside your field of view, you find yourself still on the bridge.

Then you remember that your friend, although fond of hiking, has a deathly fear of snakes, all snakes, and the last time you went hiking, she shrieked at the site of a garter snake. So you decide to see for yourself if you're dealing with a threat worth getting wet over.

Your left-brain has actually stopped to *process* the input before acting on it. The input in this case was not a visual, but rather speech, similar to text and therefore subject to *interpretation* by your brain's logic center. After all, another jump into the ravine might have gotten you hurt, and before doing that, your left-brain had to know whether it was working with good information.

The result of this process in less-than-life-threatening situations is that, although we absorb colors and patterns and graphics instantly and not analytically, when presented with speech, text or numbers we pause to analyze the data before storing or reacting to it. We have filters on the left side, and not everything gets through.

So to entice the brain to instantly absorb and then retain words, it's sometime necessary to trick the hemisphere into thinking it's dealing with right-brain type stuff. One way we do that is by turning words into music, which the right brain discerns as a pattern. Right brains like and look for patterns. That's why advertisers like jingles; jingles work so well because we don't stop to process the information before absorbing it.

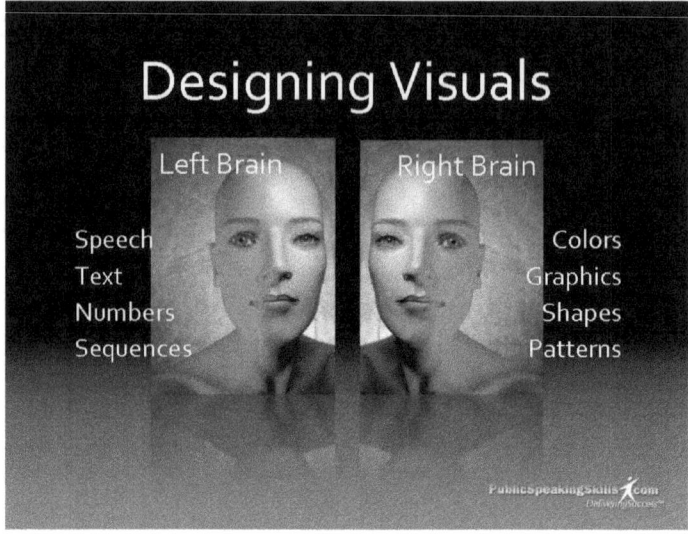

Figure 8.6 Left-brain information, such as speech, text, numbers or sequences, is not immediately acted upon as is right-brain information. Instead, it's filtered and processed.

Use Pictures, Graphs, & Images

When you think about presentations you've had to sit through, what did they mainly consist of? Were there mostly pictures, graphs, and images, or ten to twenty slides of bullet points? If you can't remember much from these last dozen productions, they were probably mostly bullet points. Left-brain filters are the gate-keepers to short-term memory, and for any input to make it to long-term memory, it must first etch into the short-term matter.

Design slides that reach out to both sides of the brain. That's where artwork can work to your advantage.

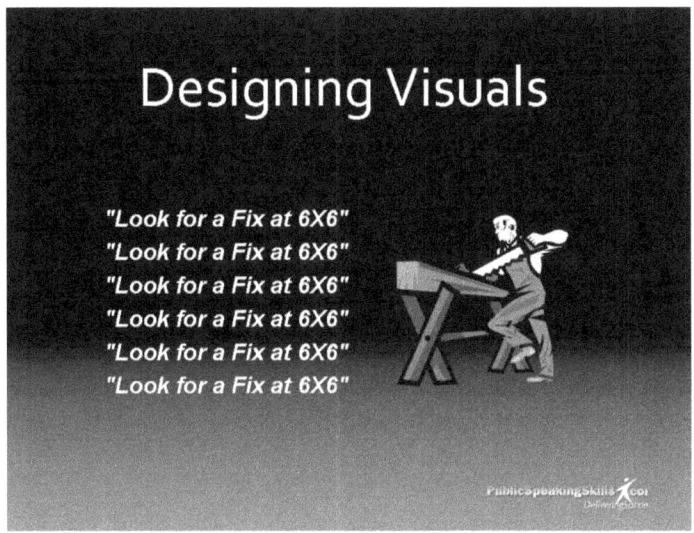

Figure 8.7 As a rule of thumb, a visual should not contain more than six lines of text nor more than six words per line. But more important than a simple rule is the concept: Keep it Simple! If you even *think* you might have too much, you do!

In Figure 8.7 the picture of the 6 x 6 creates a memory anchor to which to attach the concept in the brain. We also create a self-evident pattern with the words for even more dual-hemisphere absorption.

Points to Remember

- Favor Right-Brain information
- K.I.S.S. - Less is More
- One concept per visual
- Use proper builds
- Be colorful - Light on dark
- Avoid boring fonts
- Maintain paragraph integrity

Suggested Exercises

1. Review your last three presentations. How many times did you try to make your point with left-brain information, e.g., words and numbers, when you could have used a graph or chart instead?

2. Find three slides where you rely on left-brain information to tell your story and convert the data to right-brain info. This can include using photos instead of words, too.

3. Take one presentation and modify your slides to maintain paragraph integrity.

4. Using the Change Fonts feature from the Format menu, experiment with how changing your font from Arial or Times New Roman to something different gives your presentation a whole new feel.

Chapter 9:
Applying the Rules

In Chapter 7, you read about the ill-fated Columbia Space Shuttle and how it could have been saved if only the presenter of evidence of impending disaster had convinced the decision-making audience that a real problem existed. Here, we will use an actual slide from the Boeing engineer's presentation and show how it could have been improved using the seven rules outlined in Chapter 8.

Before we go on, however, it's essential to first note two very important things.

First, the slide you're about to see was originally brought to popular and widespread attention by none other than the distinguished Dr. Tufte mentioned throughout this text (though it had been originally obtained through the Freedom of Information Act by a Florida newspaper). Dr. Tufte was asked by the CAIB (Columbia Accident Investigation Board) to scour documents relevant to the investigation and render his opinion on whether the design of such documents may have played a role in what turned out to be some major errant decision-making. Dr. Tufte had some years earlier demonstrated that a pre-PowerPoint® era (was there ever such a time?) presentation had, through its lack of a coherent design, helped to doom *Challenger*.

Notwithstanding the respect we have for Dr. Tufte and his contributions to the art of visualizing data, he has since taken up a crusade, or perhaps *jihad*, to rally against the use of PowerPoint® in serious or technical presentations, correctly pointing out the limitations of its ability to aid true knowledge transfer when used, as it was, in this now infamous "Boeing" slide. We often joke that Dr. Tufte believes that someday, the wrong person will give the wrong PowerPoint® presentation to the wrong audience, and the world will come to an end!

Our issue with Tufte's assessment of the evils of PowerPoint® is the old one that guns don't kill people, presenters do. PowerPoint®, like a gun, or a car or a surgical instrument can be dangerous in untrained hands. But that's hardly a call for worldwide eradication. Tufte is a brilliant, charismatic performer on the platform, and can actually present well even when having his audience read along with him from one of his beautifully crafted illustrated textbooks. (An otherwise big no-no!)

For the far less-talented rest of us, PowerPoint® can be a fantastic tool that adds retention-enhancing visual interest and understanding while serving as an excellent content-management system.

The second point we need to make relates to the first, and that is this: we hold no one involved in the creation of these "Boeing" slides accountable for the tragic result of the lack of communication that permeated the management levels of NASA in 2003. We are relatively certain that none of the rocket scientists there had ever taken a professionally-developed training course in proper presentation design. Look around today and you'll be hard-pressed to find a class where you can learn what it takes to turn data into transferable knowledge – the author's firm's offerings a notable exception.

You can find a few firms that will take your ugly, unpresentable slides and make them over into pretty, un-presentable slides. But designing slides that actually work with the way the brain absorbs information is something else entirely.

The answer to the PowerPoint® problem is simple: education. Business people and rocket scientists alike simply need to be trained in the elements of presentation design before putting their PowerPoint® files on automatic and senselessly firing away at their audiences. PowerPoint® is too deeply acculturated into our professional lives to be either banned (Tufte) or considered workable without training (most businesses).

It's actually a shame that Microsoft hasn't stepped up to the plate and at least used its considerable resources to defend the good intent of its product while acknowledging the need for universal training for its users. And we're of course not talking about PowerPoint® 101, but rather Design 101, courses that would give users the required background in what works and what doesn't

150

when projecting information to human brains from the big screen.

When the developers of PowerPoint® sold their product to Microsoft in 1988, one of the stipulations of the sale was that the company remain in Mountain View, California (the Silicon Valley). Perhaps the Mountain View gang's self-imposed exile has kept them once removed from the watchful eye of Redmond, and this lack of understanding of their own product's needs is an oversight that might come back to bite them someday.

But without further adieu, let's take a look at this very real, very tragic "visual".

The "Boeing" Slide

Review of Test Data Indicates Conservatism for Tile Penetration

- The existing SOFI on tile test data used to create Crater was reviewed along with STS-87 Southwest Research data
  - Crater overpredicted penetration of tile coating significantly
    - Initial penetration to described by normal velocity
      - Varies with volume/mass of projectile (e.g., 200ft/sec for 3cu. In)
    - Significant energy is required for the softer SOFI particle to penetrate the relatively hard tile coating
      - Test results do show that it is possible at sufficient mass and velocity
    - Conversely, once tile is penetrated SOFI can cause significant damage
      - Minor variations in total energy (above penetration level) can cause significant tile damage
  - Flight condition is significantly outside of test database
    - Volume of ramp is 1920cu in vs 3 cu in for test

BOEING 2/21/03 6

Figure 9.1   Slide 6 of a 12 slide presentation to Mission Management and others. Yes, the other 11 looked just like it.

KILLER PRESENTATION SKILLS

Let's review how this slide conforms to The 7 Rules from the bottom up, and then see if there just might be a relationship between the quality of its design and its success as a knowledge transfer device:

Rule 7: Maintain paragraph integrity

It's hard to see paragraph integrity when you're only working with one slide. However, this one violates the rule by disrespecting that the viewer is going to assume the most important information will be delivered in the largest type, and probably at the top of the slide. Here, the only bit of truly actionable data is presented in the smallest font size.

Rule 6: Avoid boring fonts

Could you be more guilty of really bad design than to use Arial in black against a white background? All 28 slides in the 3 presentations designed by the rocket scientists used this comprehension-killing approach. Is it any wonder why none of the serious data stuck with the people trying to view 12 slides that all look like this? They more or less massacre the 6 X 6 rule as well, stroking 17 body text lines with an average of 8.3 (and as many as 12) words per line.

Rule 5: Be Colorful

Covered, don't you think?

Rule 4: Use proper builds

Well, you can't *mis*use builds if you don't build at all. Here, they clearly break the rule by bringing on 17 lines of text all at once, with no chance for anyone to decipher one bit of information before being hit with the next.

Parceling alone might have saved the day by bringing forth that one bit of important data with its own time and attention slot.

Rule 3: One concept per visual

We stopped counting the number of concepts when it got to 6, but the damage here is even more severe. Note that at the first dash-shaped "bullet", we're told that "Crater over-predicted penetration of tile coating significantly." But three dots later, we learn that "Conversely, once tile is penetrated SOFI can cause significant damage." So not only do we have more than *one* concept, we have *conflicting* concepts presented at the same time.

You know you're in trouble when you see the word "Conversely" in the middle of the slide. Again, the only concept that means anything at all here lies buried beneath an avalanche of other concepts.

> *"What a beautiful design! The only way it could be any better is if there were less of it!"*
>
>   - Edward Tufte

Rule 2: Less is More

When we present this slide during live presentation design classes, we set a stopwatch when it first appears and then note at what times eyeballs depart from the fray and start looking elsewhere for comfort. Some people start giving up at about 45-seconds; those determined to slug it out usually take a minute and 15. Remember that *Less is More* holds within it the 10-second rule; your visual shouldn't include more information than it takes the normal person 10 seconds or less to comprehend.

You know, if the rocket scientists had used more judicious tabbing and reduced the indents of the bullets by a half-inch or more, it is possible they could have filled the *entire* slide with words. Well, there's always next time. And finally,

Rule 1: Favor right-brain information

Here is where any hope of knowledge transfer dies in the quagmire of the slide. Of all the ways they might have presented the one set of data that means anything, the one piece of actionable information that should have bowled the executive rocket scientists over mercilessly, their one shot at slam-dunking their argument, they chose instead to ask themselves, "How can we make this information more *left*-brained".

Rocket scientists, people whose job it is to be a little more technical than using the word "significantly" five times, got this whole right-brain, left-brain thing mixed up. Instead of what might have been a simple 1-column, 2 number chart, they display the only actionable numeric data in the slide as a full blown left-brain sentence. This one act of bad design killed all chance for comprehension as surely as hot cosmic gases blowtorching through Columbia killed the good men and women inside.

Figure 9.2 All the worthwhile, actionable data in the entire slide lies in one line at the bottom, rendered in, of course, the smallest font size used. And not just the smallest, but in uber-left-brain format, all numbers and text without even using a common protocol to make clear that both "1920" and "3" referred to "cubic inches".

The slide is invisibly summed up in the very last line. In fact, the entire slide — no, make that the entire presentation — could have been, should have been thrown in the hopper and reduced to one simple graphic. One simple graphic could have said all that needed to be said about the situation to know that a catastrophe was, indeed, imminent.

Tragically, none of the points that the rocket scientists were trying to make needed to be misunderstood. Without changing any of the data or eliminating any of the information, though that certainly wouldn't hurt, the same presentation could have been given, and the audience could have agreed with their argument, if only the slides had stuck to the rules.

Columbia data by the rules

Although much has been written about how this one slide demonstrates the theory to banish PowerPoint® from all serious meetings, we take a different, and, we think, much more practical approach.

We believe, in fact, that had the rocket scientists been educated in proper presentation design, they could have made such a compelling case for caution that no one in that fateful meeting room would have thought twice about going ahead with re-entry. Used properly, the graphics capability of this simple program can convey concepts of the most complicated origin.

The first job of fixing this mess was to apply a few basic right-brain friendly touches such as color, an image, and a less than boring font. Then we tore the slide apart so that all the data on each slide was relevant to all the other data on the slide, and when we ran out of data, we went to — are you ready? — a NEW (albeit *duplicated*) slide. In the same manner that time goes by just fine even when not filled with your talking (a key concept behind The Pause), slides need not be filled with massive strings of words for them to function.

Please note that for the sake of reader interest, we've offered a synopsis of each slide to suggest its true underlying meaning. As we discuss each bullet point, we address each concept in order, but use different and more interesting language to describe more fully what the viewer has just read. This is the opposite of reading the slides, where the presenter, speaking more slowly than the viewers can read, only tells them what they by that point they already know!

Review of Test Data Indicates Conservatism for Tile Penetration

- The existing SOFI on tile test data used to create Crater was reviewed along with STS-87 Southwest Research data
  - Crater overpredicted penetration of tile coating significantly

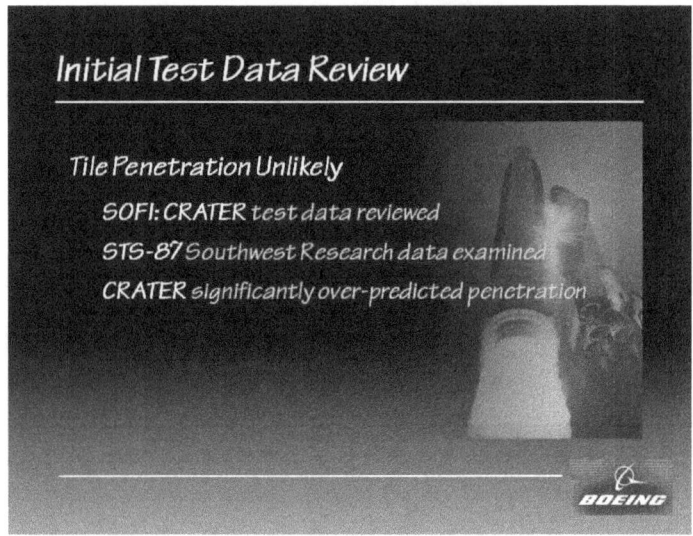

Figure 9.3 Synopsis:

"When we first looked at the data on possible damage to the orbiter from flying foam, it appeared as if it were unlikely to be severe enough to endanger hull integrity.

"When we reviewed the data from our CRATER tests and compared it with actual damage that Southwest Research found on shuttle flight #87, we concluded that the test model predicted more damage than what actually occurred."

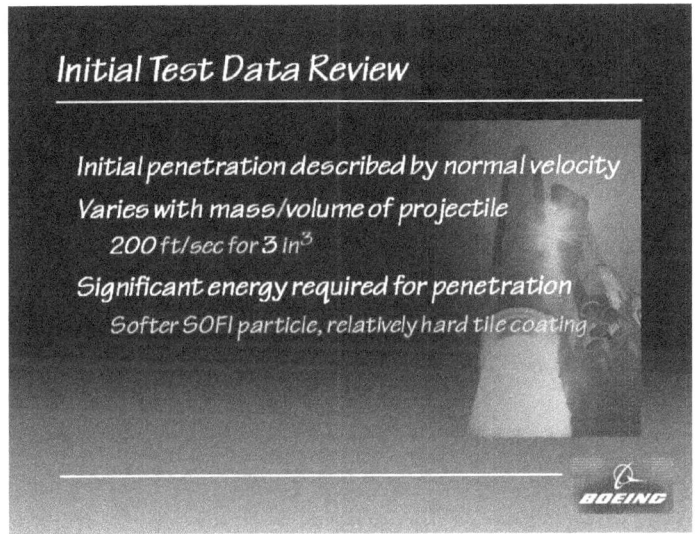

Figure 9.4 Synopsis:

"Actual damage is a function of basic physics; the speed of impact varies with, among other things, the size of the particle. The tests used a piece of foam about the size of a golf ball traveling at 133 mph.

"But our first intuition suggested that a throwaway coffee cup, even tossed from a speeding train, couldn't damage baked enamel."

Then..

158

- Test results do show that it is possible at sufficient mass and velocity
* Conversely, once tile is penetrated SOFI can cause significant damage
  - Minor variations in total energy (above penetration level) can cause significant tile damage

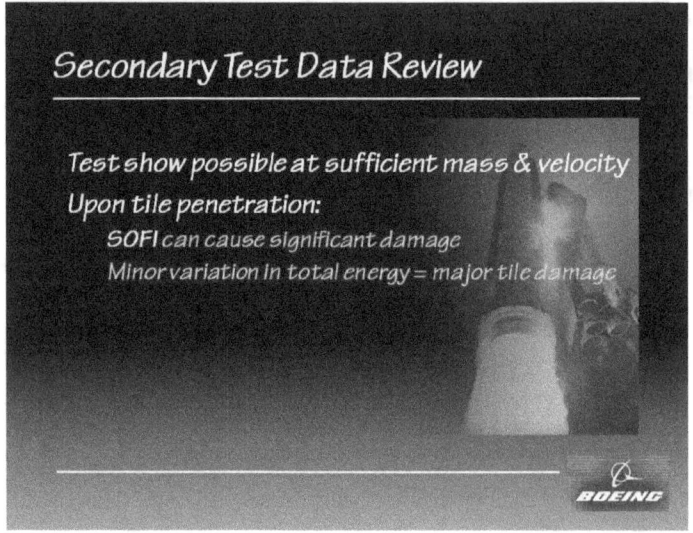

Figure 9.5 Synopsis:

"Upon further, deeper review of the data, however, we discovered that if you have a big enough piece of this foam traveling at a good enough clip, once it penetrates the tile you can actually mess up somebody's whole day."

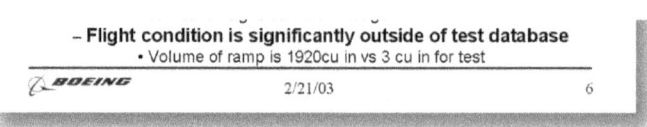

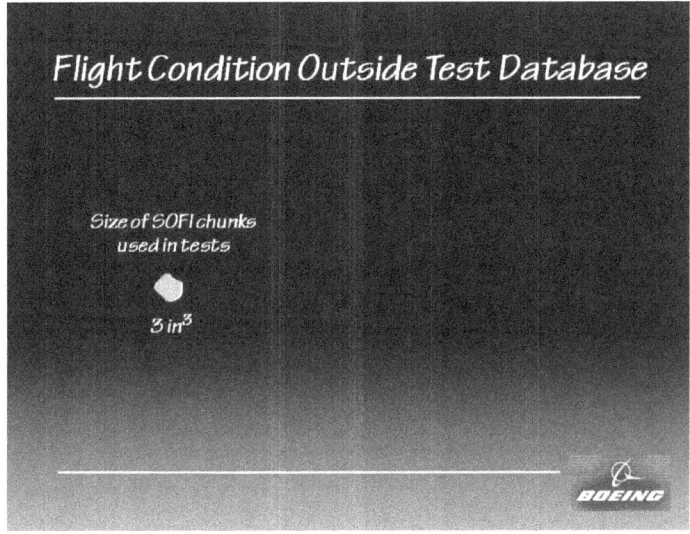

Figure 9.6 Synopsis:

"Unfortunately, ladies and gentlemen, you know all that stuff we just showed you to impress you with the breadth and depth of our knowledge? Forget it – for the situation at hand, it doesn't mean squat.

"The only thing that counts is this: Just because we shot frozen peas at the windshield all night and the windshield held...

> *"If you can't describe what you are doing as a process, you don't know what you're doing"*
>
> - W. Edwards Deming

And with a flick of the headline…

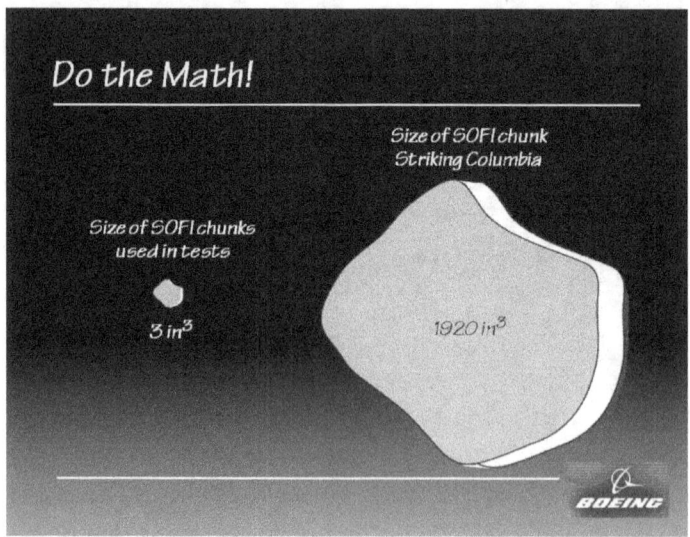

Figure 9.7 Synopsis:

"…Can we assume the same result if we shot frozen pumpkins instead?

Or you tell me, Houston: Do we have a problem?"

When we show this set of slides in class, and ask our students if anyone would have elected to bring Columbia down after seeing the argument put this way, it's usually a fait accompli — no one sides with NASA. We then ask if anyone in the room is a rocket scientist, and very few raise their hands. (Of course, when our audience was a group of brain surgeons, we had a number of alternative responses.)

The point is, of course, that one need not be a rocket scientist to be persuaded by right-brain information.

Edward Tufte would have the rocket scientists share their information with others through the use of heavily (and properly formatted) foot-noted written documents, which is an admirable approach. Not very realistic today, but nevertheless admirable.

And yet it is strikingly clear in this right-brain slide that PowerPoint® actually *can* function quite adequately when attempting to make an argument based on data, if only that data is represented in a way that is unambiguous to even the casual observer. Casual observers tend to skip the footnotes.

(The Editor holds the position that upon viewing the edited slides, one not need be a rocket scientist to come to the conclusion that the Columbia should never have been cleared for landing. On the other hand, the Editor acknowledges that many readers are actually taking up space at their current jobs).

The role of the presentation designer (and this is a role that in most cases should be assumed, at least in large part, by the presenter herself) is not to ensure that the presentation includes all the relevant data. The responsibility of the designer must be to ensure that the audience *receives* the data, and receives it in such an unambiguous way that all eyes are seeing exactly what the presenter has in mind.

Ironically, PowerPoint® is a tool uniquely suited to do just that. We believe this last slide would have sent such a message, and more strongly and more unambiguously to the assembled audience than any scholarly dissertation Dr. Tufte would have been able to assemble.

As we've mentioned before, a problem with the common PowerPoint® culture in most businesses today is the misconception that the same document can serve both functions — the projected program and the takeaway. Those two functions could not be more diametrically opposed, and yet we still see edicts from on high proscribing design rules that are meant to work for the printed form — all at the expense of deliverability from the screen.

Virtually all of the problems we see with corporate presentations can be traced to the misguided belief that somehow a software program invented to lessen the presenter's dependence on the graphics department can now *by decree* be the universal document production software for all information transfer — and that all knowledge transfer shall be conducted through ONE document, regardless of whether it's for group or individual consumption.

Could you imagine if Steven Spielberg set out to make a movie of a Steven King book, and then used the book itself as the screenplay? Would you sit through a 12-hour movie, with voice-over narration taking the place of visual images?

Points to Remember

- A properly designed onscreen presentation should never attempt to take the place of a well-researched and well-written, content-rich and grammatically correct printed document.

- A content-rich and grammatically correct printed document should never take the place of a properly designed onscreen presentation.

- Books and movies can tell the same story, but each according to the rules and structures that work for each art form. Why should presentations be considered any differently?

Suggested Exercises

Go to:www.publicspeakingskills.com/cato/Airplane.ppt

This text gives you all the information you need to make an airplane that will fly reasonably well if the audience follows the directions closely.

The text contains 289 words. Your job in this exercise is to reduce that number to as low as you can while still conveying enough information for the audience to build a flying model on the first try. Assume your audience is somewhat learning challenged, and use everything you have learned about presentation design to get that number down.

Hint: we do this as a competition in our onsite corporate classes, and the winners takes home twenty dollars (remember the $20 rule?). Winning entries are always below 50, but we know you can do even better than that!

Building a Paper Airplane

If you have a minute's worth of time you can build a paper airplane. You'll need a fresh piece of paper, preferably 8 ½ inches wide by 11 inches tall, and a stable, hard surface on which you can press firmly to ensure your creases are sharp. To begin, fold the paper in half lengthwise, and press a crease into the fold. Then, open it back up so it lies flat.

Starting with the upper right-hand corner, fold it into the center, making a 45-degree angle. Do the same with the upper left-hand corner. At this point, your project should take on the shape of a house. Now, taking each side in turn at the "eve", fold the sides once more into the center. Secure creases in these folds, also. Fold the whole thing in half along the original fold you made at the start.

Finally, create the wings by folding each folded half outward and down to the main fold. This is normally done so the wings are the same size as the fuselage. (However, larger wings make the plane more of a floater, with more lift, and smaller wings make for a faster dart that flies a smaller distance. Just experiment!) Open out into plane shape. Experiment with wing angles for the best results.

For better performance, you may wish to fold little "ailerons" into the back edges of the wings, so that the extent of the lift causes the plane to loop the loop. If you fold the flaps upwards, it will loop upwards, and vice versa. If you fold one upwards and one downwards, the plane will spiral through the air, although not for very long.

Note: To see the author's solution, go to:
www.publicspeakingskills.com/cato/airplanefix.ppt

Part III:
Putting it All Together

*"Education is not filling a bucket,
but lighting a fire."*

- William Yeats

Chapter 10:
Stand and Deliver

Now that you've culled and edited your content down to where you know your audience will give you their utmost attention, where do you position yourself when you give your talk? How do you click your slides? How do you divide your attention between what's happening on the screen and the audience?

We are rarely blessed with a perfect room setup in which to present, or even modest control over what we're given. In most hotels, for instance, it often seems that the hiring process for AV crews goes something like this:

Interviewer: *Have you ever given a presentation in front of a group before?*

Applicant: *Nope.*

Interviewer: *Have you ever wanted to give a presentation in front of a group before?*

Applicant: *Nope.*

Interviewer: *Have you ever seen a presentation given in front of a group before?*

Applicant: *Nope.*

Interviewer: *Great! You're hired.*

Although we recognize that the settings in which you are required to present are not always ideal, you still want to get as close to the ideal as you can. Where you stand in relation to the screen, the content and the timing plays a role in helping the audience receive your message.

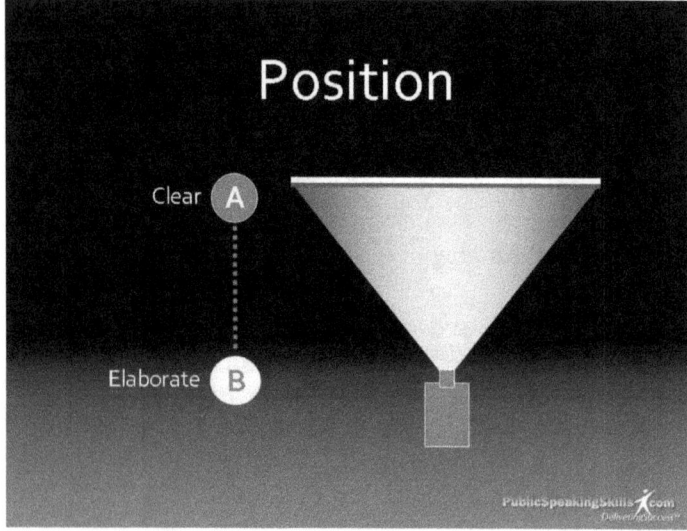

Figure 10.1 Stand by the screen to allow your audience to satisfy their curiosity about the slide when you bring up new information. Then move forward to let them know to transfer their attention to you.

For example, when you click new information onto the screen, you should be standing right inside the plane where your audience's attention will be focused. And, if you want to keep everybody in sync, stay there until you have covered all the information available to see.

Only after you and the audience have both acknowledged what's on the screen should you venture forward. As you step forward, your movement draws your audience's attention away from the screen and onto you. It is from this forward position that most of the presentation will take place.

By separating yourself physically from the screen, you help to re-enforce the notion that the screen is there to help, not replace, the presenter. Most of the words in your presentation must originate with you, from the heart, and not the screen.

It's All in Your Head

Good presentations are never memorized. They occur when you "launch" from the screen, and convert your talking points into a conversational discourse about what you know. The less scripted the presentation, the less you'll sound like a...well...*script,* and more like an expert.

In fact, that is exactly how you want to envision yourself delivering your presentation. Think about how you feel when you are talking with friends around a table over lunch. (Go ahead and add a glass of wine or a bottle of beer to that imagination.) Does that scene make you nervous? Of course not!

Some presentation experts actually encourage you to *memorize* your way to confidence in public speaking. Here's one such expert, quoted along side us in an article from the online version of USA Today:

> "Once you've settled on the verbal and visual content of your talk, it's time to start rehearsing. Take a small chunk of the material and practice it out loud 30 to 50 times. Practice it in your throwaway time — in the shower, on the way to work. Practicing 10 to 20 times makes you sound rehearsed, but 30 to 50 times makes you sound natural. By that time you've done it so much it's like a muscle memory for your throat... You don't have to think about it."

Can you imagine that? *Fifty* times? Is your life so void of other responsibilities that your can practice a slide fifty times? And why would you want to so thoroughly memorize a piece that you might only give once, and then start all over again for the next one?

Worse, as good as you might get with memorizing ninety-five percent of your presentation, when you get to that one part you don't remember, you'll freeze. And as the fear of looking foolish builds quickly, your mind will lose the ability to process, much less *recall*, the rest of the detailed information.

Wouldn't it be better if you had a system that required no memorization at all? One that simply gave your memory a shove every few moments and then let you be yourself? One that frees you up to say whatever comes to your mind at the time?

Reading is NOT fundamental

Putting meat on the bones is exactly what you, the presenter, are there for. You're not there to read the slide. The audience can do that quite well for themselves, thank you. In fact, the people who came to hear you speak can read words about 40% faster than you can speak them — 250 words per minute for them vs. 150 wpm for you.

That's another reason you don't want to have proper sentence structure on the screen — wording that just begs to be read. When you do, the problem is twofold:

You, as the presenter, will not be able to resist reading straight from the screen, because you're conditioned to do that when your brain recognizes a properly structured grammatically correct sentence.

And the audience, also being human, will do exactly the same thing. But because their reading takes less time than your speaking, by getting in their way to be *the first to know*, you are telling your audience that you really don't care very much about them. It is the equivalent of having a minivan that waits until the last minute to pull out into the road in front of you, and then proceeds to drive 40% slower than the speed limit you had been pleasantly exceeding.

TMI on the screen also leads to breaking the essential bond between audience and presenter that occurs only with constant eye contact. Unable to keep in your head all of the information flashed up on the screen, you are forced, by design, to turn your back on the audience as you read from the screen.

When your visual is so complex that it forces you to read from the screen, you can't maintain eye-contact with members of the audience. When this all-important component to proper presenting is lost, attention erodes.

Absorb, Align, and Address:

The solution, then, is to restrict the volume of information at each exposure to that which can be *absorbed* by both you and the audience in just a few seconds. The proper procedure for achieving transfer of information from the screen to the audience involves a process we call Absorb, Align, and Address.

Absorb

When new information appears on the screen, all eyes will follow it, and at this point it is not only OK, but required, for you to look to the screen also. By doing so, you "give permission" to the audience to divert their attention from you and look instead to the screen. Of course, if you have correctly limited the amount of information that appears with the next click of your mouse, that diversion will not last very long. At this point, because you are not looking at any individual in the group, you must be silent.

By the way, no, you may not look to the screen on the

laptop in front of you to grab the information. For several reasons you never want to use a laptop as a teleprompter. It's not only distracting for audience members to follow your eyes to someplace they can't see, but a main benefit of your looking to the screen each time is that it reinforces the bond between presenter and audience when each is pursuing the exact same behavior at the same time.

(A third reason not to read from your laptop is that in rare cases, usually involving graphics or video, your laptop may be displaying the images properly but the projector may not. You must know what the *audience* is seeing at all times.)

When you have absorbed the data bite, you can now think for a moment how to phrase what you want to say. This would not be expounding, but merely filling out the talking points to make a grammatically correct statement.

Align

After you and your audience have had the opportunity to take in this information, turn your attention away from the screen, and lock eyes *(align)* with a single member of the audience. This is the most difficult part, physically, to perform, as the natural tendency is to begin speaking as soon as you have formulated your statement. But delaying your vocalizing until you have locked on to a target will become second nature with not too much practice. Remember its always Lock first, then Talk. Trying to find your target as you are speaking is doing more than one thing at a time, in violation of Rule #1.

Address

Locked on, you finally can *address* the audience (one member at a time) with your version of the talking point.

Again, this address should not be just the words in the bullet point. Your words should be a coherent, complete thought that lets the audience know what the 1 to 5 word bullet point means.

You may always say more than the line on the screen, but never any less. The group will have read everything that's on the screen, so if you put words up there but don't speak to them, you insult your audience: *These words aren't important enough for me to bother with but I wanted to take up your little brains' time just the same.*

Don't Leave 'em Hangin'

You go to a presentation and watch slide after slide of footnotes and small type, or graphs with legends and data to which the presenter never refers. You're looking at all the elements on the slide trying to figure out which stuff is most important, and then the presenter never even mentions half the stuff you've read. How does that make you feel? For most people, the first slide that contains more information than the presenter talks about is the point at which they check out. They tell themselves that they can figure it out easier from the handout. (Which, of course, they trash at the first receptacle they see outside the presentation room.)

Once learned, the *Absorb, Align and Address* system is a

beautiful thing to watch. Slides designed with this system in mind never suffer from TMI, and thus never have too much for you to deal with. Your confidence is high, knowing you're never going to be overwhelmed by the information that appears with the next click of the mouse. You audience feels this too. They are forced to turn their attention to you because there's not enough information on the screen to allow them to jump to their own conclusions. By the same token, you are now able to direct all of your spoken message to the audience and not the screen.

But here's the really fun part: When you follow this simple plan for both design and delivery, almost anyone can look and sound like an expert on their subject, regardless of how much prep time they've put into *rehearsing* the presentation! We prove this during live classes by having participants deliver other participants' presentations that we have edited and revised to comply with the rules.

From the Heart

Ideally, of course, you should have a good background in the subject matter so that you can deliver a credible presentation. But if you know to what the talking points refer, and you also know that no more material than you can deliver in just a few seconds will appear with each click of the mouse, you can actually give a presentation *for the very first time* and sound like you've been doing it for years.

The Right Stuff

Because Microsoft provides you with the functionality to completely control the flow of information from the screen to the audience, we say, *"Use it!"* Employing "builds" or, as Mama Microsoft alternately calls them, "animations", is only problematic when you don't have the right equipment to advance your slides. If you have to walk up to a keyboard and strike a key six or more times per slide, you'll distract your audience.

Unfortunately, you rarely know what kind of equipment you will have until *after* you have designed your presentation. So when you choose your venue, make sure the Minimum Equipment List shakes out.

Your MEI should include some type of remote mouse, preferably of the newer radio-frequency (RF) design instead of the old infrared systems that require a line-of-sight to the receiver.

If you don't have the right equipment and are using slides with multiple bullet points (and not designed with builds), you must clear each element on the screen before moving out from the plane of the screen to expound on any one point.

With builds, you would address each of the points at length before moving on to the next. But remember, when everything comes up on the screen at once, your viewers are reading and analyzing each point, and won't pay attention to you until they've read each one and satisfied their curiosity.

So in the absence of builds, you may find yourself remaining silent for quite some time. Again, this is why you want to always look to the screen with each advance of the mouse. The minimum time for you to stay silent is the time it takes *you* to read the material on the screen. Even if you've given the presentation a dozen times and know the slides cold, you have read each new item to yourself to know how long the audience needs to satisfy their collective curiosity.

As you process each bullet point, use an open-palmed Vanna White type gesture to reinforce their attention to the next topic.

If, on the other hand, your slide uses builds, you can tell the whole story about a point before moving on to the next. Or, as with the static slide, briefly clear each point and then go back. The point is, builds still provide maximum flexibility — especially with the right equipment — so take advantage of them if you can.

A final pointer:

Any time we go to a presentation and spot a pointer on the podium, we know we're doomed. Pointers worked well for World War II generals to pinpoint bombing targets on blown-up aerial photographs of Axis industrial facilities. Today, they merely compensate for an overly complicated visual.

The problem with pointers is they are only useful if your slides are not properly designed in the first place. A pointer allows the presentation designer to get lazy.

Most of the time you only need to point when you have more than one concept on the screen at the same time. And if your slide really requires the audience to focus on a small detail, you can always use the software to do so. You can draw a circle around the item, an animated stroke underneath a word, or shade out everything on the screen except for the item you wish to highlight.

Save it for the Handout

If detailed content such as statistics or measurements with significant digits is required, the proper place and venue for that information is on the handout, not on the screen. Just be sure to give the handout *after* the presentation so your audience does not ignore you completely to read through it.

To create handouts using PowerPoint®:

- Draft your presentation with all the information you want to disburse.
- Save that and use it as your handout.
- Then make a copy and edit the presentation down to meet the rules of proper visual design.

Your audience will thank you for your brevity, and be inspired to drill down into the written piece for more information.

Points to Remember

- Never memorize your presentation. You seem *more* credible when you sound *less* rehearsed.
- If a sentence works grammatically, it does not work presentationally.
- To completely control the flow of information, use builds and carry an RF controller.
- If you feel the need to use a pointer, you have too many concepts on the slide.
- Give the handout, which contains more details than the slides, *after* the presentation.

Suggested Exercises

1. Nailing the Absorb, Align and Address process is not difficult, but' it's difficult to practice without an audience. If possible, then, find at least two volunteers to sit in on your delivering a presentation and tell them to stop you every time you go from the Absorb stage and begin Addressing before you have Aligned.

> *"The man who can think and does not know how to express what he thinks is at a level of him who cannot think."*
>
> \- Pericles

"Discovery consists of seeing what everybody has seen and thinking what nobody has thought."

- Albert Szent-Gyorgyi

Chapter 11:
The Dreaded Q & A

OK. The presentation's over. You've stunned them with your beautifully minimalist PowerPoint® slides. You've demonstrated the breadth and depth of your knowledge not with volumes of data on the screen, but with words spoken from your heart and pretty much off-the-cuff, using your slides as a *guide*. You've kept their rapt attention and controlled the entire process. And now, all of that is about to come to shuddering halt.

Welcome to Q & A.

Unlike the presentation itself, where you totally controlled the flow of information, you now find yourself having to relinquish that control to people you don't even know — people who might have their own agendas. Perhaps even people who have come armed with erroneous or downright negative information, and who are looking for a bit of the spotlight themselves.

Depending on the reason for your presentation, this audience might be composed of people who want to make you, or your company, look bad.

Hold All Calls

You've found yourself in this situation because at the beginning of your talk, you asked the audience if they would please hold all questions until the end. But was this the best approach?

For most presentations, where your purpose is to define and propose a solution to a problem, or expose and recommend action on an opportunity, it generally is best to hold all questions until the end. Given that you are probably working within a fixed time frame, it's essential that you get your entire message across. Allowing interruptions in the middle of your message can put that goal in jeopardy.

In fact, the problem with taking questions during your presentation is that, like eating certain potato chips, it's impossible to take just one. As soon as you open that door, you can't close it without alienating several people who feel that their question was at least, if not more, as relevant as the one you took.

So allowing questions at any time is a sure-fire way to lose control of the presentation process. Worse, getting off on tangents can lead to losing your focus on the information that you studied before your talk so that you could speak in a conversational, impromptu way. Better to remain in control until the message is made.

One important exception to this rule is when the purpose of your presentation is to instruct. The role of the educator is to ensure that everyone understands the skill or the information being taught, and that process is usually best accomplished when everyone is on board with the one module before moving on to the next.

In the process of handling antagonistic questions, one of the last things you want to ask is, "Did I answer your question?" The reasons for that will become clear momentarily. Conversely, in a learning environment, it's essential that the participant asking the question understands and is pleased with your answer, because you don't want him thinking about his problem when you move on to the next item in the curriculum.

For this reason, if you are there to teach, you definitely need to limit the scope of your presentation to allow for the fact that you might spend half your time dealing with questions. Of course, limiting your scope is a good idea in all presentations, but if your audience really must understand and retain what you're sharing with them, limiting is the key. If you have an hour, make sure you can complete the body of your talk in 40 minutes. No exceptions!

Neutralizing Negativity

"Words are the ambassadors of our intentions" – Susan Harrow

If your presentation is not purely instructional, and if you want to make sure you and your organization come away from your talk in the best possible light, there is a very structured process for dealing with questions. We say 'structured' because, in order to ensure it works every time, you must adhere to the exact process for every question.

To be clear, we're talking about handling questions in an environment where the audience isn't only looking for clarity. The process we're about to describe is designed for those situations where:

- Somebody in the audience tries to inject her personal agenda into the Q & A module.
- The questioner injects inaccurate information.
- The question contains highly negative wording that you certainly don't want to repeat.

In the case of the personal agenda question, you don't want to answer any question that leaves out everyone in the audience except the questioner. Your job as presenter is to continue the knowledge transfer to all throughout your time up front. When you enter into a dialogue with just one member of the audience, you immediately risk losing the interest of the rest. In this case, you must reform the question into one whose answer provides knowledge for all.

People often come to a presentation fully armed with inaccurate information. When they inject those inaccuracies into questions, you don't want to give any more credence to their words than necessary.

And when the question is a downright attack, when someone is being openly antagonistic (think of the press verses George Bush), your first and natural response might be to challenge him. Unfortunately, there's nothing gained and much to be lost in a confrontation with members of your audience. In any confrontation, people tend to choose sides. You don't need people whom you've wowed to your side during your presentation to suddenly jump ship.

It's better to be armed with a process that instantly neutralizes the threat, and puts you in a positive light.

No Spin Zone

Before we go on, it is important to note that we're not talking here about spin. Putting a spin on the question is how a politician might get out of a tight situation; rather than answer the specific question he is asked, he spins the question into one he wants to answer. This is *not* what you should do. But to be clear you understand the difference, here's an example of how a question can be 'spun' into something different:

Reporter: Mr. President, troops have been in Iraq for five years. When are you going to admit that the fight is lost and just bring them home?

George Bush: *The question of when the troops come home is on the minds of many Americans. No American family wants their sons or daughters in harm's way, and they don't want their futures to be up in the air. In fact, all American families feel ill at ease when their children's future is unclear, whether they're in the armed forces, or in college, or looking for work in a stressed economy.*

That is why it is so important that Congress act quickly to make the tax cuts of 2001 permanent. It's only in a low-tax environment that employers dare to expand their factories and offices, which is where full-time employment comes from. Give Americans lower taxes, and I guarantee you their children's futures will be secure.

Spin has its place, but not in the types of environments you're likely to encounter in the business presentation world. Two more things you never want to do in Q & A are:

1. Make up an answer because you don't know
2. Lie

Lying or making up an answer is almost always counterproductive. Some people ask questions to which they already know the answer simply to see if you do, too. You've just spent forty-five minutes building credibility with your expert presentation, and it all dissolves in a minute when your questioner discovers that you're blowing smoke.

Rather than giving a false or potentially inaccurate answer, it is much better to say that you don't know, but will get the answer to them later. But you don't have to actually say the words, "I don't know". One phrasing we like and use often is:

"You know, I'm not the best person to answer that question. But I work with Bob, whose job it is to know exactly what you're asking. If I can get your contact information when we're finished, I'll see to it that Bob gets back to you".

By saying you're not the 'best' person to answer that question, it implies that you *could* give an answer, but that you would feel better if the questioner got the *best* possible answer.

Of course, if you find yourself unable to answer a large number of the questions posed, it begs the question of whether or not you were right person to give that presentation in the first place. Next time, it might be better to send Bob!

The Process

So let's first take at look at the process of your response, and then discuss each step. Here is the sequence of events – and remember, following this sequence for every question is the key to controlling the entire Q & A process.

- Model and ask for questions
- Select with open palm and *Listen!*
- Break visually
- Rephrase or repeat
- Begin with questioner, spread it around
- Don't end with questioner
- Ask for other questions

Model and ask for questions

When you begin the Q & A section, let people know how you want them to respond. This is best done by modeling the behavior you are looking for.

Simply raise your hand and ask for questions. You can say, *"Any questions?"* which sometimes does the trick, but because it's a closed-end question, a null response can make it awkward to proceed. An open-end question is more inviting.

"That's the end of the presentation. At this point, most people have questions. What are yours?"

By suggesting that most people have questions, some in the audience who do have questions but might be afraid to ask realize they're not alone. Keep in mind that some people are reluctant to ask questions because they're afraid they might not have been listening during the topic and will look foolish if you actually covered the topic at length. Still others will want to wait until someone else asks the first question so they can judge whether or not their question sounds stupid.

At times when you really want audience members to ask questions but no one is willing to pull the cord, you can always prime the pump:

"I gave this presentation two weeks ago in Chicago, and the first question I got was…"

Now no one needs to go first.

Select with open palm & *listen*!

When someone finally does raise her hand, using the action you have modeled, select them with an open palm.

Don't point. Few people like to be pointed at. An open palm is much more gracious and inviting.

And try to avoid making references to the individual such as, "The gentleman in the third row". More than one speaker has been embarrassed to discover too late that he had made a gender-recognition error, and suffered the retort, "I ain't no gentleman, sonny!"

While on the subject of don'ts, don't refer to the questioner by name unless you know the name of *every* person in the room. The unnamed can feel slighted. The exception to the rule is if the questioner is someone everyone in the room knows, such as the CEO.

Avoid saying, "Good question." With the possible exception of the NextGen crowd, who need to be praised for their every action, responding to every question with 'Good question' gets old very quickly. And what happens when you get a question that's obviously not a good question, perhaps even downright stupid? The first time you don't say 'Good question', the questioner says to himself, "What exactly is wrong with *my* question?"

So after selecting with an open palm and perhaps a "Yes..." you now need to do something rarely done in Q & A, and that is *listen!*

The most common mistake presenters make is to try to answer before they've heard the entire question.

In 2007, a young person answering a question in front of a few hundred people found her performance viewed by several million just a few days later, and it wasn't because she did such an excellent job. The teenage beauty pageant contestant was asked a question to which she gave a totally inane, rambling and senseless answer, because, as was clear in her response, she only heard the real question after she was halfway through her pathetic parade of disjointed half-answers. If you've seen the video, you know whom we're talking about, and you know that if you don't take the time to listen, you can find yourself on YouTube tomorrow!

The Atomic Theory of Q & A

The most important reason for listening to the question is so you hear not only what is asked, but what the central topic of the question is.

Think of the question as an atom. An atom is, of course, composed of a nucleus, containing protons and neutrons, surrounded by a sphere of spinning electrons. The electrons are negatively charged, the protons are positively charged, and the neutrons, are, well, neutral. Your job is to find the neutrons.

In a hostile Q & A environment, your mission is to break through the negatively charged field surrounding the nucleus, and get to the center. In the nucleus you will find positively charged particles, but you don't want to rely on them too heavily because you don't want to be accused of spin. What you really want to concentrate on are neutrons. Neutrons are neither positive nor negative; they have no "charge".

Essential Point: You need to listen for what is at the uncharged nucleus of the question, after all the personal agenda items, and the inaccuracies, and the *negativity* have been stripped away. Because it is to this nucleus, where you will find the "neutrons", that you will address your answer, not necessarily the question as it was posed.

This will make more sense when we get to actual examples of questions and what their nuclei are in just a bit. For now, understand that even though you might think you know what the question coming at you is going to be, there is no need to jump the gun. Listen. Remember that audiences don't really hear what you say, but rather what you just said. Same applies to you.

Break visually

While the questioner is talking, you must maintain direct eye contact with him. Letting your eyes wander at this point sends the message that you're not really listening, and it can make the questioner defensive and be much harder on you than if you let him know you can take anything he throws at you, eye-to-eye.

But as you begin the next step, it's critical that you break visually and deliver your next words with another individual, preferably on the other side of the room.

Rephrase or Repeat

This is by far the most critical part of this process. At the very least, unless you're in a very small group and everyone's heard the question and it's a relative softball, you want to repeat the question. Repeating has two benefits. For the audience, it assures that they know what you're giving the answer to because the question is coming from the same voice and direction that they've been listening to throughout your presentation.

Nothing is more frustrating than when someone from the front row asks a question in a meek or quiet voice and the speaker launches into an answer, even though no one in the back heard the question. The answer tends to be something like, *"Oh my god, we'd never do that again. The last time we tried that, ten people died! Next question?"*

For you, repeating gives you a little more time to think about the answer. But once you learn this technique, we suggest that as long as you're going to repeat the answer, you might as well rephrase it.

Rephrasing every question has its advantages. First, rephrasing, when done using the nucleus method, demonstrates to the audience that not only did you listen to the question, you listened deeply enough to give the most complete answer. And by complete we mean giving an answer of a much wider scope than the original question asked for. It reinforces their perception of you as an expert on the topic, and shows the audience that you care enough about them to include everyone in the answer, not just the person who asked the question.

With the nucleus method, you are continuing the knowledge transfer process that you began with your presentation, and you don't leave out the rest of the audience as you address only the more narrowly focused subject of the original question.

But it is also in the rephrase that you have the opportunity to strip away any negativity or issues or inaccuracies that you would otherwise be reinforcing if you simply repeated the question.

Finally, by rephrasing *every* question, you don't send the signal that you're only rephrasing the hardball questions, because for some it might appear that you are spinning.

An example

You raise your hand, look at one person in the audience, and announce:

"That's the end of the presentation. At this point, most people have questions. What are yours?"

A person in the third row, who has been almost sneering at you throughout your talk, raises her hand. You look her in the eye, offer her your open palm, and say, *"Yes?"*

She unloads:

"What's going on at your plant in Smallville? I heard there was an explosion there and people were killed, and that it wasn't the first time something really bad has happened there. Have you guys just thrown OSHA out the window?"

Now here is a question that would not do you much good to repeat. If you said, *"The woman wants to know if we've thrown OSHA out the window at our Smallville plant"* in a nice clear, loud voice, you would definitely be reinforcing the notion that you're doing something bad in Smallville. Not a good plan.

Instead, ask yourself what the nucleus of the question is. What, when you strip away the negativity and erroneous material, is the question really about? The nucleus never has any negative or positive connotations whatsoever; it is simply what the question is *about*.

Discovering the nucleus may take a little practice. But once you've mastered it, as most people with *The Skills* have done, you'll likely find yourself answering every question this way.

Anytime the question of accidents or explosions or deaths or injuries come up, what the question is really about is *safety*. Safety is the nucleus. Though the words "accident" or "injuries" imply a negative, the nucleus of the question — the word 'safety' — is neither negative nor positive. By discovering the nucleus, then, you instantly neutralize the question, and you don't repeat or reinforce images that work against you.

The next step is to break visually with the person who asked you the question, and find another person with whom to lock eyes. And yes, during Q & A all the same rules of presentation apply, especially the one that says if your eyes aren't locked your jaw must be. You first rephrase the question.

"So what is the safety record at our plant in Smallville?"

Pay close attention here: note that your rephrase does not begin with the words, *"What the woman wants to know* is what's the safety record..." Nor does it begin with, *"The question is..."* Both of these phrases would beg the hostile questioner to interrupt you and say, "No, that's *not* what my question was! My question was..." It's also the reason you break visually with the questioner and state the question you're going to answer, *"So what is the safety record..."* to another person. The very first words out of your mouth need to be the question you are going to answer, with no attributions of any kind.

Begin with questioner, spread it around

But now you do want the questioner to know that you are not avoiding her, so you begin your answer with an opening point to that person:

"Yes, we did have a mishap at our Smallville plant recently, and thank God no one was killed." This erases the inaccurate information in the question. You now break visually again and continue with another audience member:

"As you might have seen on the news, we did incur some injuries, and we are all saddened when any MegaManufacturing employee meets harm in any way. What I can tell you is this: the Smallville safety record is in the 98th percentile of all plants in our industry, a record we are extremely proud of."

And to yet another person:

That's what makes any incident, no matter how small, a sad event for the people who strive so hard to keep our work environment the very safest it can be."

And to another:

"We have already begun a very extensive in-house investigation of the cause of the accident, and it is through investigations such as these that we learn how to prevent similar mishaps in the future, and not just here but in our other plants across the country."

By discovering and addressing the nucleus, *safety*, you are now free to expound the scope of the question to include not just what happened at Smallville, but to include how seriously the firm looks out for the well-being of all of its employees everywhere. So a question that started out with both negative and erroneous information turns into an opportunity to spread the good word about your firm, and nobody feels he or she has been spun.

Don't end with questioner; ask for others

And now, making sure you are looking at anybody but the questioner, you ask:

Any other questions?

The reason you never end with the questioner is that you want to avoid giving him the opportunity for a rebuttal. You don't want to invite a *"Yeah, but…"*

Again, spin is about how you *avoid* answering the question you were asked. This process is, instead, about *rephrasing* the question you are given into a question that will serve the widest possible audience with the greatest amount of knowledge transfer. It keeps you from losing the rest of the audience as you get into a narrow dialogue with only the questioner.

Your answer to the nucleus question still needs to be honest and direct. You can't lie or make things up. You can't switch the topic to one of your choosing as you do with spin.

The nucleus method assures that your answer will be on target to the questioner, because you have taken the time and effort to determine what the question is really about. But the nucleus method also allows you to give answers to the group, spreading it around as you had done during your presentation, and everyone stays on board.

When you follow these steps with every question, you never get caught in a situation where you are tripped up by an antagonistic party. Your audience will actually gain respect for your expertise. And, by taking the time to rephrase, you broadcast to the audience that you have, indeed, *listened* to the question.

For the past fifteen years, we have been not only teaching the nucleus method to tens of thousands of class participants, we have been using it all day long in all our trainings.

In our presentation skills classes, the Q & A module comes at the end of the day. During a typical class day, because we employ a very facilitative approach to training, it's not unusual for us to field thirty to forty questions by the time we get to Q & A. After explaining the nucleus method, it's not uncommon for us to get a raised eyebrow here and there, as at first glance to some the process smacks of something between spin and avoidance.

We'll then ask the audience if they can guess how many questions they've asked us during the day, and most come close to the real number. We then ask them how many questions we either avoided or spun, the universal reply is always none, because indeed we're in the business of making sure the questions we answer have the widest possible audience base.

When we tell them that we apply the nucleus method to *every single question* they ask, and give them examples from the day, we see little lights go on as they suddenly come to realize that they had been *processed* all day long and never once realized it! The nucleus method works because it actually gives audiences more than what they asked for.

Let's look at a few more examples to help your minds get in the nucleus groove:

1. *Why do all your products cost so much?*

Who hasn't been asked this one before? You get questions on cost or price in many different forms, but what is at the nucleus of any question on cost? That's right — Value. So you *could* repeat the negative and say:

Why does are stuff cost so much? Or, you could go to the nucleus:

How do we value our product line? Or,

How do we establish the value of our products? Or simply,

What is our value proposition?

In each case, you would begin your answer referring back to the original question. For example,

"Yes, our products often do sell at a premium to others available in the marketplace. But we are proud of the fact that the high quality of our merchandise is not only reflected in much higher resale value than any other line, but our products have a 30% higher mean time between overhaul than the next closest competitor.

So although our initial purchase price is, indeed, higher than most others, we have by far the lowest total cost of ownership."

2) *You've failed to meet completion deadlines before. What makes you think you'll succeed this time?*

Quick! What is the nucleus? It's certainly not either failure or success, because the nucleus never has any connotations — bad or good. The key word here is 'before', and it's at the root of a lot of tough questions.

When you really listen to the question, and you hear the word 'before', it's likely that the nucleus of the question is 'history'. History is history — it's what it is. And so:

"What's our project completion history?" Or,

"What's our history on new projects?" Or maybe even,

"So what's our history here?"

Your answer would be whatever the truth is. Remember, you're not spinning the facts here. All you are doing is looking to strip away the negatives in the *question*, so that you don't reinforce bad or erroneous allegations that put you or your organization in a bad light. And if you have examples of projects that were completed on schedule or even ahead of schedule, rephrasing the question this way allows you to include positive examples even as you acknowledge some negative examples in the past.

3) *Who came up with this ridiculous plan?*

The nucleus here may not be obvious, but the root of the question is fairly common and leads to a rephrase that can be used in a broad spectrum of responses. Initially, the 'who' part of the question begs to focus the blame on an individual. It might as well be, *"What idiot came up with this ridiculous plan?"*

Again, the nucleus here can be difficult to picture until you've done this mental exercise several times. But what the question actually invokes is, "How did you decide to do it this way?" or, "Why are you doing it this way?"

So our real nucleus, after stripping away all the layers of blame assessment (who? what idiot?) and judgments about the solution (ridiculous plan), is found in a *decision* to which somebody or some group came.

Ultimately, people at all levels in all organizations make decisions, and from those decisions flow actions. Although there are good decisions and bad decisions, the word 'decision' or 'decide' has no inherent connotations. It's a perfect nucleus, and can be used in a plethora of rephrases.

"How did we decide on this plan?" Or,

"What was the decision process here?" Or,

"Why did we decide to do it this way?"

Nothing personal - it's just business.

The next two examples show how you can move the focus from an actual individual to a more general answer that doesn't get bogged down in personalities.

4) *Aren't you a bit inexperienced for this position?*

This is a simple one. 'Inexperience' obviously has bad connotations that you wouldn't want to repeat, but it's really just the flip side of 'experience', which sounds good but at essence is neither good nor bad. So instead of repeating or rephrasing, "Am I inexperienced?", you just turn it around:

"So what's my experience?" Or, taking the concept of experience to a deeper nucleus,

"What are my credentials in this area?" Or simply,

"What are my credentials?"

Sometimes, individuals will try to use your presentation as a forum to air their personal grievances. These are people you need to cut off at the knees, because nothing will send your audience heading for the exits like a discussion between you and someone about whose problems they could care less. But believe it or not, you can still neutralize this situation without getting confrontational. So when you get:

5) *Why didn't I get the raise I was promised last year?*

Most likely, nobody else in your audience really wants to hear about Sally's failure to make the next pay grade. Instead of answering, *"Sally, you didn't get a raise because you're a monumental screw-up!"* you can look for the nucleus and rephrase accordingly.

And here, Sally is asking about money. Specifically, money tied to work, or wages, which we also know as that totally connotation-less but broadly encompassing term 'compensation'. And because it's also a 'why?' question, the good old nucleus standby 'decision' comes into play, so we handed the rephrase on a silver platter:

"How de we make compensation decisions?"

Or, using another super connotation-free term 'policy',

"What is our compensation policy?"

And in this case the answer is easy, because Sally actually is a monumental screw-up. So after breaking visually with Sally to give the rephrase, you turn back to her and begin:

"Well Sally, as you know, our employee policy manual specifically states that in order for employees to keep their jobs, they must report to work a minimum of 3 days per week every week that they are not on vacation or sick leave.

Then after pausing and turning to a new target:

"Management has been quite lenient with some employees in

allowing them to stay on even though they've averaged less than 3 days per week, but we've had difficulty in granting these people the standard 5% raise that otherwise comes with an employee's one-year anniversary."

You have taken a personal agenda question and by simply rephrasing to the nucleus, you have spread the knowledge of what is expected and what benefits await all employees who play by the rules, and thereby kept your entire audience's attention.

Using the nucleus method, and adhering to the steps in strict sequences, there are no questions that will put you in bad light or make you appear anything less than an expert on the subject. However, it's not an easy method to learn unless you practice it constantly, and practice it often enough for it to become second nature. Just like *Lock, Talk, and Pause*, which is not second-nature now, the more you employ it the more quickly it will become so. And the multiple benefits of feeling secure going into any Q & A session make the work worthwhile.

Final pointers

As is true with so many aspects of the presentation process, when it comes to the rephrase, less is definitely more. Shorter rephrases signal that you are sharp enough to discern the essence of the question; longer rephrases risk sounding like an attempt to avoid or spin.

If you find yourself struggling to come up with a nice, clean, short rephrase, here's a silver bullet:

"*What about…*" [Insert nucleus]

'What about' can neutralize virtually any hardball question without your even having to spend time coming up with a clever rephrase. Just be sure to put equal emphasis and tonality on both 'what' and 'about' as you pose your rephrased question; overemphasizing 'about' makes the phrase sarcastic.

So, if you're hit with a question such as:

"Hasn't your new drug already killed dozens of people?"
   "What about *our new drug Thorelepdazine?*"

Haven't you lied about Iraq enough?"
   "What about *Iraq?*"

"Is it true you're going to lay off 10,000 at your Syracuse plant?"
   "What about *Syracuse?*"

'What about' is a silver bullet because you can use it anywhere in zero time. But you definitely don't want to overuse it, because your audience will eventually figure out what you're doing. You can use it more than once, though, as long as you take the time and effort to more gracefully rephrase the majority of your questions. Better to keep it in your holster until you find yourself stuck and have to pull it out.

Forewarned is forearmed

The last thing we want to leave you with is that the best way to answer any question you might get is to know what the questions coming at you will be ahead of time.

When you do, you can have the best answers already vetted and prepared. In many cases, its easier than it sounds. It simply requires a little data management.

There is a classic episode of Seinfeld where George Costanza is at a Yankees management cocktail meeting. When a coworker catches George stuffing himself with shrimp he quips, "Hey George, the ocean called; they're running out of shrimp." Slow-witted George cannot think of a comeback until later, while driving home.

His comeback is, "Oh yeah? Well, the Jerk Store called, and they're running out of *you*." He shares this with Jerry and the group back at Jerry's apartment. Although Jerry and friends offer better retorts, George becomes obsessed with recreating the shrimp eating encounter so that he can flog his coworker with the comeback. But when he gets the chance, he of course is outwitted again, and finds himself once more obsessed with coming up and delivering a new comeback. How many times have you said to yourself, *"What I should have said was…"*

The point is, most questions you get generate two answers: the one you actually give at the time, and the one you wished you had given after having the chance to think about it for a while.

If you are one of many people in your organization giving the same presentation to different clients over a period of time (for example, a national product rollout), you can do what many large companies do: manage a database of all the questions ever asked at Q & A. Chances are, after a short period of time, all the different questions that will ever be asked at your presentations shall have been asked already, even though you, working alone, might not have fielded them yet.

If everyone on the presentation team logs every question into a database and you peruse the database before every presentation, you will have the luxury of knowing everything that might be slung at you. Of course, your database not only logs the questions, but it also has the answers that were given, and even the answers people came up with later (the answers they *wished* they'd have given – think George).

Remember, although presentations are not about practice, practice, practice, they are about prepare, prepare, prepare. The same definitely applies to Q & A.

Going into Q & A with a database of what's likely to be asked, and answers massaged with the power of hindsight? You couldn't be better prepared.

Points to Remember

- Getting confrontational during Q&A is usually a losing proposition.
- Neutralize negativity by finding the nucleus of the question. Restate the question using the nucleus. Keep the rephrase short.
- Answer the question without lying, making up an answer, or spinning it into a different question.
- The process for Q&A is:
    - Model and ask for questions
    - Select with open palms and *Listen*!
    - Break visually
    - Rephrase or repeat
    - Begin with questioner, spread it around
    - Don't end with questioner
    - Ask for other questions
- Keep a database of questions so you can use those answers to prepare for future Q&As on the same presentation.

> *"If you had to identify, in one word, the reason why the human race has not achieved, and never will achieve, its full potential, that word would be: 'meetings'."*
>
> - Dave Barry

Suggested Exercises

Determine the real nuclei of these questions, and craft the simplest, shortest rephrase. Remember, your rephrase will not contain any attributions — only the words of the question you are about to answer.

1. Isn't it true that you don't follow through on your commitments?
2. Aren't your so called 'facts' really unsubstantiated?
3. Why so many injuries in just the last six months?
4. Why do you let some customers pay in 60 days when our terms spell out a penalty for over 30?
5. Why did you discontinue the 360 Series?

1)History 2)Research 3)Safety 4)Credit policies 5)Product line decisions

Appendix A

Opening to Martin Luther King's *I Have a Dream*

Let us not wallow in the valley of despair,

I say to you today, my friends.

And so even though we face the difficulties of today

and tomorrow,

I still have a dream.

It is a dream deeply rooted in the American dream.

I have a dream that one day this nation will rise up

and live out the true meaning of its creed:

"We hold these truths to be self-evident,

that all men are created equal."

I have a dream…

that one day on the red hills of Georgia,

the sons of former slaves

and the sons of former slave owners

will be able to sit down together at the table of brotherhood.

I have a dream...

that one day even the state of Mississippi,

a state sweltering with the heat of injustice,

will be transformed into an oasis of freedom and justice.

I have a dream...

that my four little children will one day live in a nation

where they will be judged NOT by the color of their skin

but by the content of their character.

I have a dream *today!*

I have a dream that one day, down in Alabama,

with its vicious racists,

with its governor's lips dripping with the words

of "interposition" and "nullification"

– one day right there in Alabama

little black boys & black girls will be able to join hands

with little white boys & white girls as sisters and brothers.

I have a dream *today!*

Appendix B

Opening to Clinton's 1997 Inaugural Speech

My fellow citizens:

At this last presidential inauguration of the 20th century,

let us lift our eyes

toward the challenges that await us

in the next century.

It is our great, good fortune

that time and chance

have put us not only on the edge of a new century,

in a new millennium,

but on the edge of a bright new prospect

in human affairs.

A moment that will define our course,

and our character

for decades to come.

We must keep our old democracy

forever young.

Guided by the ancient vision of a promised land,

let us set our sights upon a land

of New Promise.

The promise of America was born in the 18th century

out of the bold conviction

that we are all created equal.

It was extended and preserved in the 19th century,

when our nation spread across the continent,

saved the union,

and abolished the scourge of slavery.

Then, in turmoil and triumph,

that promise exploded onto the world stage

to make this,

the American Century.

And what a century

it has been.

America became the world's mightiest industrial power;

saved the world from tyranny in two world wars

and a long cold war;

and time and again,

reached across the globe to millions

who longed for the blessings of liberty.

Along the way,

Americans produced the great middle class

and security in old age;

built unrivaled centers of learning

and opened public schools to all;

split the atom;

and explored the heavens;

invented the computer

and the microchip;

and deepened the wellspring of justice

by making a revolution in civil rights for African Americans

and all minorities,

and extending the circle of citizenship,

opportunity,

and dignity

to women.

"Grasp the subject; the words will follow"
– Cato the Elder

The *Very* Quick Reference Guide

Chapter 1 - A Wiring Problem   pg. 11
- Increased heart beat, decreased cognitive function, slowed time perception, sweating, flush face & dry mouth are all normal bodily reactions to fear.
- Working less will improve your outcome.
- Slow down! Give the audience time to absorb each point.

Chapter 2 - Seeing Eye to Eye   pg.27
- Aerosol Eyes increases the frequency of new fear stimuli.
- Not looking someone in the eye equates to not telling the truth.
- Your discomfort and anxiety are contagious to your audience.

Chapter 3 - Lock, Talk & Pause   pg.39
- L, T & P reduces the brain's need to complete new threat calculations, thus reducing the call for adrenaline and restoring cognitive ability.
- Lock eyes. Talk to one person through the completion of a thought.
- Pause before engaging the next person.
- Instead of managing endless word tracks, make the next pause your constant priority. Concentrate on only the *very* next thing you're going to say.
- The larger the group, the more will perceive your eyeing them.

Chapter 4 - Power of the Pause   pg. 55
- The pause is the heart of all great speech.
- Benefits: 1) Your audience hears what you said, 2) Prepares them to hear what you say next, 3) Gives time to prepare your next thought.
- The pause in speech is equal to the paragraph break in print.
- Pausing every few words is OK. Pause at the end of each thought.

Chapter 5 - Passion   pg. 69
- Lock eyes on one person before you begin to speak.
- Talk to one, only one, person at a time no matter how many.
- People don't come to hear you speak; rather, to hear your passion.
- Use meaningful gestures, volume, interesting tone & inflection.
- At all times, be yourself.
- When all else fails, smile.

Chapter 6 - Organizing Your Presentation   pg. 89
- You have 30 seconds to let them know this is going to be different.
- Use a formula that grabs attention in the beginning, directs their attention to a pre-designated solution through the middle, & wraps it up into a neat bundle at the end.
- Presentation less than ½ hour? Skip the Agenda.
- Let them know exactly where you're going from the beginning so they can put everything you say into a preformed context.
- Give them evidence that they can relate to & shows a direct benefit.
- Close with a call to action that keeps the presentation in their minds.

Chapter 7 - Introduction to Design   pg. 105
- To convince, content form is as critical as the content itself.
- Humans have a pervasive & inherent need to be "the 1st to know".
- Your audience won't wait for you to explain.
- Limit content to no more than 10 seconds with each mouse click.
- The less on the screen, the more value you, the presenter, add.

Chapter 8 - The 7 Rules   pg. 125
- Favor Right-Brain information
- One concept per visual
- Be colorful - Light on dark
- Maintain paragraph integrity
- K.I.S.S. - Less is More
- Use proper builds
- Avoid boring fonts

Chapter 9 - Applying The 7 Rules   pg. 147
- One file can't serve as both a document to read and set of visual aids.
- Books and movies can tell the same story, but only in their own way.

Chapter 10 - Stand & Deliver   pg. 167
- Don't memorize! *Less* rehearsed equals *more* credibilty.
- If a sentence works grammatically, it does not work presentationally.
- To completely control the flow of information use builds & RF mouse.
- If you need to use a pointer, you have too many concepts on the slide.
- Give the handout, which contains more details than the slides, *after*.

Chapter 11 - Q & A   pg. 181
- Model and ask for question
- Break visually
- Begin w/ questioner, spread it
- Select with open palms and *listen*!
- Rephrase or repeat
- Don't end with questioner

INDEX

A

accident 17, 105, 192-3, 213
agencies 118-19
agenda slide 89, 213
ancestor 15-16, 213
animations 129-30, 174, 213
answer 12, 27, 147, 181-7, 189-90, 193-7, 199-200, 202-5, 213
anxiety 22, 26, 36, 38, 40, 46, 213
applaud 63, 213
arms 22, 36, 68-70, 213
attention 4, 21, 29, 35, 45, 62, 65, 89-90, 101-2, 108-10, 112-13, 121-2, 165-6, 170-1, 173-5
audience members 17, 41, 47-8, 59, 108, 111-12, 118, 120, 171, 186, 193, 213
audience's attention 71, 88, 95, 167, 201, 213
audience's brains 80, 125, 213

B

Bang 88, 99-100, 102, 213
behaviors 2-5, 22, 31, 33-4, 44, 51, 57, 171, 186, 213
  new 52, 81, 83
billboard 118-19, 213
blood 14-15, 33, 213
body 7, 11, 13-15, 18-19, 24, 32-4, 38, 42, 52, 70, 100, 133, 181, 213
  upper 68
Boeing engineer's presentation 145, 213
Boeing slides 146-8
bond 48, 71, 114, 169, 171, 213
boss 19, 33, 64, 106, 121, 213
brain 3, 13-17, 20, 23, 29, 32-3, 41, 45-6, 49, 52, 55-6, 77, 80, 139-43, 147-8
  right 126, 129, 139-41
brain surgeons 104, 158
break 21, 35, 50, 59, 67, 150, 185, 188-9, 192-3, 205, 213
bridge 139-41, 213
bullets 42, 75, 126, 142, 150-1, 213
  silver 201-2
business 2, 47, 55, 93, 97, 107, 147, 196, 199, 213, 217

C

calm 21, 33-4, 213
captivating 58, 94, 112, 213
change 18, 24, 32-4, 72, 74, 127-8, 213
charisma 3, 61, 213
charts 93, 113, 131, 136, 144, 213
classes 2, 29, 42, 45, 53, 79, 147, 158, 213
  live presentation design 151
  presentation skills 79, 195
Clinton, Bill 3-4, 58-62, 65-6, 209, 213
colors 32, 49, 125-6, 128-9, 139-41, 153,

208, 213
Columbia   103-4, 152, 158-9, 213
company   17, 19, 36, 39, 96, 136, 148, 180, 214
company history   89, 214
components   25-6, 30, 214
concepts   20, 23, 50, 102, 117, 123, 126, 130-3, 143-4, 150, 153, 176-7, 199, 214
confident   34, 72, 74, 93, 214
confrontation   183, 214
connotations   197-8, 214
content   2, 7, 51, 56, 64, 71-2, 83, 88, 106, 110, 112-13, 116, 120-2, 127, 165-6
content-originator   117-18
context   56, 91-3, 96, 214
control   20, 108, 117-18, 130, 165, 174, 177, 179-80, 214
conversational approach   25, 214
copy   60, 118, 125, 127, 129, 176, 214
cue   71, 120, 214
cultures, western   25, 27, 79
curiosity   89, 108-9, 113, 166, 174, 214

D

death   12, 14-15, 36, 38, 91, 140, 192, 214
design   7, 39, 103, 112, 115, 132, 134, 146-7, 170, 173-4, 214, 219
  bad   149, 152
  good   130
digest   55-7, 111, 130, 214
discomfort   22, 36, 38, 76, 214
documents   118-19, 133, 146, 160, 214
Duplicate Slide   122, 127, 214

E

edges   70, 162, 209, 214
editor   94, 159
education   2, 4-5, 147, 164, 214
effort   11, 71, 81, 128-9, 132, 195, 202, 214
energy   17, 22, 33, 45, 68-9, 71, 125, 214
engagement   76, 214
entertainment   115-16, 214
environments   46, 182, 184, 188, 214
equipment, right   174-5
event   13, 17, 48, 108, 112, 133, 185, 193
evidence   88, 92-4, 101-2, 104, 106, 145, 214
examples   96, 189, 196-7, 199, 214
experience   113, 199, 214
experiment   51, 144, 162, 214
experts   105-6, 167-8, 173, 190, 201, 214, 218
expose   18, 42, 71, 180, 214
eye contact, holding   25-6, 30-1, 38, 40-2, 79, 214
eyes   7, 22, 25-9, 31-2, 38, 40, 44, 47, 49-51, 60-1, 65, 75-6, 79, 170-1, 191-2
  lock   40, 49, 81, 171,

192

F

FAA 90-1, 215
Favor Right-Brain Information 139, 144
fear 15, 18, 20, 25, 36, 38, 42, 141, 168, 215
fear memory 15-16, 215
Fiorina, Carly 58
fight 12, 14, 33, 68, 183, 215
file 16, 49, 82, 99, 118-19, 121, 147, 215
focus 2, 21, 45-6, 134, 176, 180, 198-9, 215
fonts 123, 128, 144, 149, 215
Forethought 117, 215
fugitive 75-6, 215

G

Gerard 75-6, 215
gestures 22, 59, 68-70, 81-3, 215
Gore 63-4, 215
grabber 88-91, 93, 100, 102, 215
Grand Masters 58, 215
graphics 113, 120, 127, 139, 141, 152, 171, 215
graphs 120, 127, 131-2, 134, 136, 142, 144, 172, 215
group 1, 3-4, 12, 14, 19-20, 26, 29-31, 36, 51, 57, 66, 78-9, 116-17, 165-6, 215-16

H

handouts 55, 78, 99, 115-16, 119, 129, 133, 137, 172, 176-7, 215
hang time 50, 82, 215
Harrow, Susan 181
Hasselbeck, Elisabeth 58
head 65, 76-7, 117, 167, 169, 215
headline 87-8, 92, 122, 125, 127, 158, 215
heart 14, 17-18, 106, 173, 179, 215
home 15, 18, 49, 138, 161, 183, 215
hormones 13-14, 17, 215
humans 13, 27, 37, 51, 95, 108, 113, 121, 125, 128-9, 139, 215
hyperlink 136, 138
hypothalamus 13-14, 42, 215

I

images 97, 138-9, 142, 153, 171, 192, 215
inaccuracies 182, 189, 191
individuals, group of 35, 40, 42-5, 47, 66, 76, 78, 199, 215
inflection 22, 29, 72-4, 81, 216
input 38, 139, 141-2, 216

J

jerk 127, 216
Jerry 203, 219
job 4, 26, 32-3, 39, 43-4, 99, 106-7, 116-17, 133, 159, 182, 184
jokes 23, 110, 146, 216
jump 14, 32, 70, 140-1,

173, 189, 216

K

Kennedy, John F. 58, 60-2, 216
Killer Presentation Skills 4, 216
Kimball 75, 216
knowledge transfer 107, 151, 160, 182, 194, 216

L

laptop 35, 171, 216
laugh 23, 216
lectern 70-1, 216
left-brain information 142, 144, 216
legends 134, 172, 216
listeners 22-3, 50, 55, 60, 82, 91, 97, 133-4, 136, 216
location 104, 125, 127
Lock 7, 39-40, 42, 45, 48-9, 51-2, 54, 59, 69, 83, 171, 201, 215-16

M

magazine 115-16, 119, 139, 216
Mark Twain 11, 56, 84, 95, 122, 216
master 23, 54, 56, 59-60, 62, 64-5, 78, 216
material 50-1, 93, 106, 112-14, 116, 126, 168, 173, 175, 216
members 39, 48, 76, 110, 123, 170, 172, 182-3, 216
memorize 74, 168, 177, 216

Microsoft 117, 124, 147-8, 174, 216
mimicking 106, 216
module 181-2, 195, 216
money 28, 47, 135, 200
Most presenters 19, 41, 71, 77
Mountain View 117, 148, 216
mouse 75, 112, 170, 173, 175, 216
movements 68, 167, 216
movies 75, 116, 160-1, 216
muscles 68, 216

N

NASA 103, 105, 147, 158, 216
negativity 189, 191-2, 204, 216
neutrons 188-9
newspapers 54-5, 57, 217
Next Steps 99, 189, 192, 217
Noonan, Peggy 67
nucleus 188-9, 192, 194, 196-201, 204, 217
nucleus method 190, 195-6, 201, 217
numbers 12, 14, 26, 32, 53, 60-1, 80, 95, 120, 126, 141-2, 144, 150,

O

observers 35, 48, 115, 217
on-screen 71, 116, 130, 161, 215, 217
organization 47, 97, 118, 181, 197-8, 203, 217
OSHA 191, 217
outline 88-9, 92

P

pace   22, 46, 57, 72, 120, 123, 130, 217
page   1, 37, 50, 54, 90, 114, 116, 118, 123, 125, 135, 217
palms, open   185-7, 191, 205
paper airplane   162, 217
paragraph   54-6, 217
paragraph integrity   123-5, 144, 149, 217
participants   2, 29, 35, 41-2, 48, 95, 173, 181, 217
passion   67-8, 72, 74, 78, 81, 93, 217
patterns   113, 126, 139-41, 143, 217
pause   7, 24, 39-41, 43, 46, 48-9, 51-4, 56-64, 66, 73, 81, 83, 114, 141, 153
  next   81
  one-second   24
  timed   56
  working   46
pause method   49, 217
pausing   55, 59, 62-3, 65, 76, 200, 217
paying attention   35, 110, 217
perception   6, 17, 24, 46, 190, 217
person   12, 14, 30, 32, 40-1, 43-6, 49, 53, 57, 64, 70, 76-8, 81-2, 103, 190-3
  average   110, 122
  best   184-5
  next   40-1, 43, 46, 49, 53
personal agenda question   182, 201
Physical Behaviors   7, 9, 217
pictures   56, 72, 95, 97, 118, 120, 139-40, 142-3, 198, 217
plane   162, 167, 174, 217
pockets   69-70, 217
podium   15, 17, 31, 70, 175, 217
pointers   175, 177, 217
power   3, 7, 10, 33, 42, 53, 61, 136, 204, 217
PowerPoint   49, 82, 113, 117-18, 124, 128, 146-8, 153, 159, 176, 217
presentation   35, 37-9, 57-8, 87-8, 90-1, 101-2, 114-18, 120-2, 128-9, 132-4, 165-8, 172-7, 179-83, 190-2, 203-5
presentation delivery   107, 218
presentation delivery skills   107
presentation design   106-8, 147, 153, 161, 213, 218
presentation designer   133, 159, 175
presentation experts   168, 218
presentation process   71, 180, 201, 218
presentation room   172, 218
presentation skills   64, 213, 218
presenter   20, 22, 34, 41, 90, 106-9, 111-12, 114, 116-18, 121, 129-31, 145-6, 159, 169, 171-2
president   4, 27, 59, 62,

64, 183, 218
President Clinton 3, 59, 65, 218
problem 20, 28, 32, 34, 47, 59, 70, 74, 77, 91-3, 105-7, 118, 125, 160, 180-1
problem/opportunity 88, 92, 102
product 39, 47, 98, 117, 119, 147-8, 196-7, 218
PublicSpeakingSkills.com 2, 107, 113, 218

Q

Q&As 20, 205, 218
questioner 182, 184-5, 187, 189, 193-5, 205, 218

R

Reagan, Ronald 58
reason 2, 13, 37, 44, 59, 88-9, 101, 105, 169, 171, 180-1, 193-4
recommendation 92-3, 218
relationship 57, 63, 218
rephrase 185, 189-92, 194-5, 197-202, 204-5, 218
result 28, 30, 33, 37, 140-1, 158, 218
retention 136, 138, 218
right-brain information 123, 142, 151, 159, 218
rocket scientists 103-5, 147, 149, 151-3, 158-9, 218
room 28, 30, 33-4, 39, 43-4, 49, 87, 89, 101, 109, 158, 187, 189, 218
rules 7, 31, 42, 67, 76, 106, 113, 115, 123, 136, 145, 149-50, 152-3, 161-2, 171
Rules of Visual Design 7

S

scan 28, 34, 219
scope 181, 190, 194, 219
screen 29, 71, 82, 99, 109-16, 121, 125-6, 129-30, 133-4, 136-9, 148, 160, 165-7, 169-76, 179
screenplay 160, 219
script 74, 82-3, 128, 167, 219
seconds 26, 41-2, 45, 57, 89-91, 101, 110-11, 113-14, 121-2, 151, 170, 173, 219
sentences 55, 62, 72, 87-8, 119, 219
sequences 80, 142, 185, 219
Shakespeare 114-15, 219
shrimp 203
signals 1, 13, 42, 47, 66, 191, 219
silence 23, 63, 65, 219
Skills 2-5, 18-19, 21-2, 25-6, 29-30, 34, 41-2, 44-5, 50-1, 58, 60-2, 71, 77-8, 81, 219
slides 71, 75, 82, 104-13, 120, 122-7, 129-34, 136, 144-5, 149-53, 158-9, 165-6, 168-9, 172-7, 179
  new 109, 127
  reference 136, 138
SlideShow mode 82, 219
smile 55, 66, 79-81, 219

snakes   139-41, 219
SOFI   104-5, 219
speakers   1-2, 4, 11, 22, 26, 29-34, 36-7, 40-1, 44-5, 54, 56, 59-61, 68, 70-1, 74
 great   3, 25-6, 56, 58-9, 61, 63, 67
 speaking   3, 5, 12-13, 26, 29-31, 36, 38, 40-3, 48-9, 51, 56, 61-3, 74, 111, 171
speech   2, 8, 20, 23, 40, 44, 46-7, 49-51, 54, 60-5, 77, 80, 141-2, 219
spin   100, 183-4, 188, 194-5, 201, 219
spray   30, 32, 219
START listening   19, 23, 55-6, 219
statistics   91, 94-5, 102, 176, 219
steps   1, 21, 35, 37, 51, 100, 123, 126, 139, 167, 185, 195, 201, 219
stick   43, 75, 89, 100, 128, 136-7, 219
stimuli   18, 34, 42, 139, 220
stop   19, 23-4, 40, 46, 48, 55-6, 59, 63, 140-1, 177, 220
story   41, 57, 90-1, 95-6, 116, 144, 161, 175, 220
subject   33-4, 61, 72, 75, 141, 173, 187, 190, 201, 212, 220
Synopsis   153-8, 220

T

text   23, 49, 54, 80, 82, 125-7, 139, 141-3, 145, 150, 152, 161, 220
textbook   54, 57, 220
thinking   1, 18, 21, 33, 37, 43, 46, 51-2, 76, 89, 101, 112, 141, 178, 220-1
threat   13-14, 16, 18, 41, 77, 79, 141, 183, 220
time slows   46, 220
tone   2, 22, 29, 72-4, 220
topic   2, 47, 68-9, 75, 81, 115, 186, 188, 190, 194, 220
trust   25, 28, 79, 220
truth   19, 21, 23, 27, 31, 38, 52, 79, 95, 197, 207, 220
Tufte   138, 145-7, 160

V

value   24, 78-80, 93, 121, 138, 196, 220
Verdana   128, 220
viewers   110, 149, 153, 174, 220
visual   32, 123, 126, 129-31, 134, 141, 143-4, 148, 150-1, 170, 220
visual aids   118-19, 121, 129, 220
voice   36, 72-3, 105, 190-1, 220
volume   22, 29, 34, 57, 72, 74, 106, 116, 118, 126, 170, 179, 220

W

white space   55, 136, 220
woman   59, 79, 191-2, 0
www.publicspeakingskills   31, 49, 60; 65, 82, 162

ABOUT THE AUTHOR

J. Douglas Jefferys began his platform-training career in 1981 with Commodore Business Machines. There, Doug was challenged to present what was then a hobbyist's concept - the PC - as a viable new consumer product. To best showcase its features and functionality, Doug learned BASIC and built from scratch what is now acknowledged to be the first computer-based on-screen presentation.

Years *before* Windows, Doug was helping to create the ground rules for successful computer-based presentation techniques. Today, in addition to training thousands of satisfied participants in proper public speaking skills, Doug continues to develop and edit dynamic on-screen presentations for top executives at many Fortune 500 companies.

Doug's previous work...*And Your Point Is?* - *How to Stop Killing Your Clients with PowerPoint Poisoning*, is an entertaining look at the state of business presentations today, and what you can do to improve the breed. It is also a great primer on one of Doug's passions, namely good design.

Doug has also produced and stars in two popular DVD's. *Conquering Death by PowerPoint* teaches the 7 Basic Rules of Visual Design, and demonstrates quite clearly how to craft slides that deliver your message the first time, unequivocally. And the Amazon.com Number 1 Best Seller on the topic, *90 Minutes to Killer Presentation Skills*, is now in its Second Edition. The several YouTube trailers have been viewed over 1,200,000 times.

Doug is a sometime contributor to the *Wall Street Journal*.

KILLER PRESENTATION SKILLS

KILLER PRESENTATION SKILLS

Please note:

If your position involves giving presentations to others outside your organization, you know how important referrals can be to the success of your business. In the publishing business, it works the same way, only referrals take the form of *reviews*.

If you found the content of this book useful, and worthy of a four or five star review, would you be so kind as to share your experience with others?

If so, simply go to Amazon.com or B&N.com and type in the search term *Killer Presentation Skills*.

By scrolling to the bottom of the page you will arrive at the area where they ask you to share your comments. We really appreciate your time in doing this – all we ask is that you keep within the spirit of the saying, "If you like it, tell others, if you don't, tell us!"

We trust that you did enjoy learning the skills, which, when implemented faithfully, will actually make a significant difference in your career and your life. We urge you practice these skills at every opportunity until they become, as they surely will, your second nature.

Thank you for your time and interest.

And please stop by and visit us at:
Killer Presentation Skills!

KILLER PRESENTATION SKILLS

KILLER PRESENTATION SKILLS

SPECIAL OFFER!

Don't think that just because you've read the book and done the exercises that your self-improvement has to stop there!

Now you can continue the process by acquiring the DVD, *90 Minutes to Killer Presentation Skills*, for an especially low price available exclusively to purchasers of KPS – The Book.

See the author in action as he physically demonstrates the skills you've learned – and do as so many viewers do: watch it or listen to it again just before each big presentation you give. Read the reviews on B&N.com or Amazon, then go to:

www.publicspeakingskills.com/pages/Store-DVD-Videos.htm

After you've pressed Add to Basket, type in the promo c(

UNTILKARS

www.ingramcontent.com/pod-product-compliance
Lightning Source LLC
Chambersburg PA
CBHW070940230426
43666CB00011B/2501